Clean, Well-Lighted Sentences

Clean, Well-Lighted Sentences

A Guide to Avoiding
the Most Common Errors
in Grammar and Punctuation

Janis Bell

W. W. Norton & Company

NEW YORK   LONDON

For information about permission to reproduce selections from this book,
write to Permissions, W. W. Norton & Company, Inc.,
500 Fifth Avenue, New York, NY 10110

For information about special discounts for bulk purchases, please contact
W. W. Norton Special Sales at specialsales@wwnorton.com or 800-233-4830

Manufacturing by RR Donnelley, Bloomsburg
Book design by Wesley Gott
Production manager: Julia Druskin

Library of Congress Cataloging-in-Publication Data

Bell, Janis.
Clean, well-lighted sentences : a guide to avoiding the most common
errors in grammar and punctuation / Janis Bell. — 1st ed.
p. cm.
Includes index.
ISBN 978-0-393-06771-2
1. English language—Sentences—Problems, exercises, etc.
2. English language—Grammar—Problems, exercises, etc.
3. English language—Errors in usage. 4. English language—Rhetoric.
I. Title.
PE1441.B43 2008
428.2—dc22

                                                            2008021345

W. W. Norton & Company, Inc.
500 Fifth Avenue, New York, N.Y. 10110
www.wwnorton.com

W. W. Norton & Company Ltd.
Castle House, 75/76 Wells Street, London W1T 3QT

 2 3 4 5 6 7 8 9 0

To all the modifiers in my life who positioned themselves right next to me and never budged. I'm grateful for the loyalty and definition.

Contents

Preface

Another grammar book? Why?

You've seen grammar books before—you may even own one that you pull out now and again, when you're uncertain about a sentence you wrote. Chances are, however, that you close that book pretty soon after you open it because you don't find the answer to your question. In fact, you can't figure out even how to look for the answer to your question because the text is comprehensive and filled with terms you've long forgotten.

English is your native tongue. Or it's not, but you know it well enough to be dreaming in it. You don't need a book that teaches grammar from the ground up. All you need is a guide that answers the questions you have from time to time, an explanation of the problems that typically crop up when you're writing sentences. Some relate to grammar (*Is it **who** or **whom**, **will** or **would**, **it's** or **its**?*); some relate to usage (*Is it **lie** or **lay**, **affect** or **effect**, **everyday** or **every day**?*); some relate to punctuation (*What belongs here—*

a comma or semicolon? Dash or hyphen? Single quotes or double?). Whatever the question, this book answers it in a way that will make sense to you.

How can I make that claim when I don't know you and I've never seen your sentences? Unless you're very different from the thousands of people I've taught over the last three decades in both academic and business classrooms, I do know you and I have seen your sentences. I know where your grammar and usage errors hang out. I know where your punctuation gaffes live. I can tell you exactly what these characters look like and the fragrances they wear. After reading this text, you'll be able to spot a mistake from around the corner. You may even be able to smell it.

Of necessity, this book contains grammar terminology, but it defines all terms in an introductory section and defines them again when they appear in a chapter. It discusses each issue, rather than just listing rules. It presents many sample sentences, incorrect and correct, so that you can see the concepts in action. It asks—and answers—the questions you're likely to have. It gives you a quiz to take at the end of each chapter, as well as answers to the quizzes, so that you can see what you've learned and what you still need to work on. It turns on the floodlights and even makes you laugh.

Finally, this book increases your confidence, which is key to writing well. I wish I could just sprinkle some self-assurance on your cereal in the morning and watch your sentences transform by the afternoon. But, alas, there's no such product on the market. We all have to make it from scratch by strengthening our skills. That's what you'll be doing as you work your way through this text.

Once you can produce clean, well-lighted sentences, you'll approach every writing project with a can-do attitude. I'm not promising that you'll ever like to write (few people do); I'm saying that you'll be able to write in a way that commands respect—from you and from your readers.

C'mon now, turn the page, scan the terminology, and jump into a chapter, any chapter. When you encounter one of your own sentences there, you'll wonder how many others slipped into this book when you weren't looking. It's time to keep an eye on them, don't you think?

—*Janis Bell*

Grammar Terminology

Parts of Speech

noun a word that names a person, place, or thing. Nouns can be concrete (*Josephine, Alabama, spinach*) or abstract (*fear, integrity, attitude*).

pronoun a word (*she, he, it, they, who, that, which, myself*) that stands in for/refers to a noun

verb or
verb package a word (*eat, ate*) or group of words (*has eaten, had eaten*) that depicts the action associated with a subject

modifier a general term for any descriptive word or group of words (adjectives and adverbs)

adjective a word (*delicious*) or group of words

(*which is delicious*) that describes a noun or pronoun

adverb   a word (*quickly*) or group of words (*in two minutes*) that describes a verb (*eat*) in terms of how, when, where, or why

preposition   a word that often conveys direction or position (*in, on, to, from, under, over, between, among*), but not always (*by, for, of*). Prepositions combine with a noun, pronoun, or noun equivalent to form a phrase (*by the way, to him, in writing*).

gerund   an action word ending in **ing** that functions as a noun (*eating is my favorite pastime; I enjoy eating*). Gerunds are noun equivalents.

infinitive   the source from which all verbs come, beginning with **to** and ending with an action word (*to eat, to relax, to converse*). Even though infinitives look like verbs, they don't function as verbs. They do other jobs: they can serve as nouns (*to nibble is enjoyable; to scarf up is divine*), in which case they are noun equivalents; or they can serve as adjectives (*to finish* *this meal, one must have a large appetite*), in which case they are part of a phrase that describes a noun or pronoun.

participle   an action word ending in ***ing*** (*debating*) or ***ed*** (*digested*) or an irregular form (*forgotten*). On their own, participles do not function as verbs. They can be part of a verb package, when preceded by an actual verb (*am eating, was digested, had been forgotten*). Or they can be adjectives, when placed next to a noun (*debating team, digested food, forgotten plan*).

Sentence Roles

subject   a noun, pronoun, or noun equivalent representing a person, place, or thing connected to a verb (an action). Usually, a subject is located to the left of a verb:

Josephine receives a lot of mail.

She is admired by her friends.

Talking on the phone is her favorite pastime.

Occasionally, a subject follows a verb (in sentences that begin with prepositional phrases, for example):

On the line is <u>Josephine</u>.

At the center of the debate is <u>Josephine</u>.

Always, however, the subject is the answer to the question "who or what?" before the verb. For instance, when you ask "Who or what receives a lot of mail?" (in the first sample sentence), the answer is ***Josephine***; when you ask "Who or what is her favorite pastime?" (in the third sample sentence), the answer is ***talking***; when you ask "Who or what is at the center of the debate?" (in the final sample sentence), the answer is ***Josephine***.

object a noun, pronoun, or noun equivalent that is not serving as a subject. Although there are several kinds of objects, it's not necessary to distinguish among them; all you need to know is that they are not subjects. (Being able to identify a subject is key to achieving subject-verb agreement.)

verb or
verb package

a word or group of words depicting the action associated with the subject

clause

a group of words containing a subject and verb. A clause can be independent (meaning it is capable of standing alone as a sentence) or dependent (meaning it isn't capable of standing alone as a sentence, even though it contains a subject and verb).

Independent clause:
Josephine receives a lot of mail

Dependent clause:
Because Josephine receives a lot of mail

Dependent clause:
Josephine, who loves talking on the phone

phrase

a group of words that does not contain a subject and verb

Prepositional phrase:
On the phone

Infinitive phrase:
To finish the conversation

Participial phrase:
Often dialing incorrectly

Clean, Well-Lighted Sentences

Chapter 1: Case

Case refers to the form of a noun or pronoun. Remember, a noun is a word that names a person, place, or thing—either concrete (*Josephine, Alabama, spinach*) or abstract (*fear, integrity, attitude*). A pronoun is a word that stands in for/refers to a noun (*she, he, it, they*).

Nouns

Nouns don't change form when they serve as subjects and objects. **Josephine**, for example, remains **Josephine**, no matter where she shows up:

> *Josephine eats anything that isn't nailed down.*

> *Food is irresistible to Josephine.*

In the first sentence **Josephine** is a subject; in the second sentence **Josephine** is an object. In both roles she remains **Josephine**, because she's a noun.

The only time that nouns change form is when they become possessive, to show ownership. The possessive form of a noun always involves an apostrophe, and it often (not always) involves an *s*. To determine where to place the apostrophe and whether to add an *s*, first type the noun. It may be singular or plural—that doesn't matter. Just type it:

> *child* singular
>
> *children* — plural
>
> *class* — singular
>
> *classes* — plural

You'll notice that ***child*** and ***class*** are singular, while ***children*** and ***classes*** are plural. Again, that doesn't matter. What does matter is the last letter of the word. Ask yourself, "Does this word end in the letter *s*?" If it does <u>not</u>, you make the word possessive by adding <u>an apostrophe and an *s*</u>:

> *child's*
>
> *children's*

If the word <u>does</u> end in an *s*, then you add <u>only an apostrophe</u> (no *s*) at the end:

> *class'*
>
> *classes'*

If you follow this guideline all the time, you'll never be wrong.

There is an alternative, however, when the noun in question is a person's name ending in the letter *s*. Some writers choose to add an apostrophe and an *s* to make a noun like that possessive. The name **Charles**, for example, can be made possessive in two ways:

> *Charles'*

> *Charles's*

That's all you need to know when you're making one noun possessive.

What do you do when two nouns own something? If you've written two nouns and each of them owns something separately, you need to make each noun possessive:

> *Josephine's and Charles' opinions often conflict.*

If two nouns own something jointly, you make only the second noun possessive:

> *Josephine and Charles' friendship has weathered many differences of opinion.*

Pronouns

Unlike nouns, pronouns do change form according to the roles they play—subject, object, and possessive. For examples, let's return to Charles and Josephine:

Subjects: *He eats to live, while she lives to eat.*

Objects: *To him, food points to life; to her, life points to food.*

Possessives: *His approach to food is practical; her approach is passionate.*

Here's a full list of pronouns in subject form:

I

you — Same

he

she

it — same

they

we

who

Here's how pronouns look in object form:

me

you — Same

him

her

it — Same

them

us

whom

Note: *You* and *it* remain the same, in subject and object form; all others change.

Usually, when you have to choose between the subject and object form of a pronoun, the sentence contains all the words you need, to help you make your decision. Inside comparative statements, however, words are often missing (they are understood). Consider these examples:

I am shorter than he.

There's no one I look up to more than him.

Why is *he* correct in the first sentence and *him* correct in the second? Because of what's understood. The first sentence is an abbreviated version of "I am shorter than he is." The second sentence is an abbreviated version of "There's no one I look up to more than I look up to him."

A comparative statement can convey different meanings, depending on the case of a pronoun. For example,

I like hummus more than he.

I like hummus more than him.

The first sentence means "I like hummus more than he likes hummus." The second sentence means "I like hummus more than I like him." You see the importance of using the right case?

The last part of this pronoun story concerns possessive case. When pronouns become possessive, here's how they look:

my

your

his

her

its

their

our

whose

Note: Possessive pronouns do not contain apostrophes.

Your and *You're* • *Its* and *It's* • *Whose* and *Who's*

Your, *its*, and *whose* are possessive. *You're*, *it's*, and *who's* are contractions for *you are*, *it is*, and *who is*. If you typed *you're*, *it's*, or *who's*, ask yourself whether you mean *you are*, *it is*, or *who is*. If not, drop the apostrophe and check the spelling.

The following sentences are correct:

> *You're not thinking of adopting a cat, are you?*
>
> *Your action may have repercussions.*
>
> *It's not a good idea to own a cat if you have allergies.*
>
> *Its fur will make you sneeze.*
>
> *Who's responsible for the allergy attack—you or the cat?*
>
> *Whose fault is it that you are sneezing?*

Who and Whom

When you need to choose between *who* and *whom*, you're usually at the beginning of a clause—that is, you're about to write a group of words that includes a subject and verb. Go ahead and write the clause. Then, identify the verb (the action). Next, look to the left of the verb, to see what the subject is (ask yourself "Who or what, to the left of the verb, is connected to the verb action?"). If there's no word, other than *who*, doing the job of the subject, then keep *who*. That's what *who* does—it serves as a subject. If another word serves as the subject, use *whom*.

In sum, use *who* when an upcoming verb needs a subject; use *whom* when an upcoming verb already has a subject (a noun or pronoun other than *who*). This guideline holds true for any situation calling for *who* or *whom*. It doesn't matter whether the sentence ends in a period or a question mark. (It also doesn't matter when the group of words coming up contains no verb, which happens occasionally. If there's no verb, you can't have a subject, which means that *who* is out of a job and *whom* is in order.)

The following sentences are correct:

> *Josephine, who usually has strong opinions about everything, gets confused at election time.*

> *She never knows whom she should vote for.*

> *Who will do the best job?*
>
> *Whom do most people trust?*

> *How does anyone know whom to believe?*

- In the first sentence, *who* is correct because the upcoming verb *has* needs a subject.

- In the second sentence, **whom** is correct because the upcoming verb **should vote for** already has a subject (**she**).

- In the third sentence, **who** is correct because the upcoming verb **will do** needs a subject.

- In the fourth sentence, **whom** is correct because the upcoming verb **do trust** already has a subject (**people**).

- In the last sentence **whom** is correct because there is no verb coming up (**to believe** is not a verb; it's an infinitive).

A confusing situation can arise if a **who** or **whom** clause contains another clause within it. The embedded clause can be seen as an interruption of the **who** or **whom** clause. Here are two examples:

> *Josephine is the one who I think should run for office.*

> *She is someone whom most people feel they can trust.*

- The first sentence calls for **who** because the verb **should run** needs a subject, regardless of the interruption **I think**.

- The second sentence calls for **whom** because the verb **can trust** already has a subject (**they**), regardless of the interruption **most people feel**.

Although neither of those sample sentences requires punctuation, it's easier to see the grammar involved if commas are inserted around the embedded clauses:

> *Josephine is the one who, I think, should run for office.*
>
> *She is someone whom, most people feel, they can trust.*

If you ignore the interruptions for a moment, you'll see clearly that **who** is the subject of **should run** and **they** is the subject of **can trust**.

Reflexive Pronouns

Reflexive pronouns—pronouns ending in **self**—are correct only when they reflect the subject of the clause they are in. For example, **myself** is correct only in a clause whose subject is **I**; **yourself** is correct only in a clause whose subject is **you**; **itself** is correct only in a clause whose subject is **it** (or a noun representing a thing).

The following sentences are correct:

> *I told myself that I would begin my project well before its due date.*
>
> *You must work on your project by yourself.*
>
> *The project itself is not the problem; getting started is what's so difficult.*

The typical mistake that people make is to use a reflexive pronoun where a regular pronoun belongs. This error often occurs in clauses that involve more than one person; it also occurs in phrases that begin with **like**. For example,

I

Josephine and myself have been talking about this project for a long time.

me

The task was originally assigned to Josephine and myself.

me

A seasoned analyst like myself should have no problem with the work.

A newcomer like herself may need assistance.

Do you see the errors?

• In the first sentence, **myself** should be **I** because it is part of the subject.

• In the second sentence, **myself** should be **me** because it is part of the object.

• In the third and fourth sentences, **myself** and **herself** should be **me** and **her** because they show up inside a phrase, not a clause. Remember, for a **self** pronoun to be correct, it must reflect the subject of the clause it appears in. How can it do that if it's not in a clause?

Case before Gerunds

Most often when an action word ends in **ing**, it is part of a verb package (*am writing, were revising, has been studying, will be graduating*, etc.) and there's no reason to think about case (case doesn't pertain to verb packages). But action words ending in **ing** can show up in other roles, one of which is the role of a noun. When an action word ending in *ing* serves as a noun, it's called a gerund. Take a look at the gerunds in these sentences:

> *Writing can be gruesome.*

> *Revising requires patience and stamina.*

> *My grades do not reflect the studying I did.*

> *I look forward to graduating.*

Can you see that **writing**, **revising**, **studying**, and **graduating** are serving as nouns? In the first two sentences, **writing** and **revising** are subjects; in the third and fourth sentences, **studying** and **graduating** are objects. Subjects and objects are roles filled by nouns, right? It's important that you recognize a gerund as a noun because sometimes you'll need to use a possessive word to the left of it, and that won't make sense unless you understand that you're dealing with a noun. Here are some examples:

> *Josephine's name has been in the tabloids lately, mostly for her going on dates with a popular screen star.*

> *Josephine's cavorting with a star could lead to her moving to Hollywood.*

> *It could also lead to his moving out of Hollywood.*

Another way to understand why you need the possessive case before these gerunds is to replace each gerund with the word *action*:

Josephine's name has been in the tabloids lately, mostly for her action.

Josephine's action with a star could lead to her action.

It could also lead to his action.

You may be thinking, "I don't need to know this—I don't write sentences like those." You don't? How about these:

We will appreciate your returning the completed application to us as soon as possible.

The work will not proceed without management's signing the contract.

I am fascinated by the company's earning significant profits four years in a row.

- The first sentence is saying "We will appreciate your action."

- The second sentence is saying "The work will not proceed without management's action."

- The third sentence is saying "I am fascinated by the company's action."

Surely, these contexts are familiar to you. Now, you'll know how to handle them.

QUIZ ON CASE

Below is a letter to Josephine, written by someone who just read this chapter but didn't quite understand all the material. Your job is to edit the letter for case only. That is, look at all the nouns and pronouns to see what form they are in. If they are correct, leave them alone; if they're not, fix them.

Dear Josephine:

1   I just finished reading a chapter whose focus is largely on you. I feel I should know you well by now but, between you and I, you're still pretty much of a mystery.

2   I have several questions for you:

3   What exactly is your relation to Charles? Is he just some guy who you like to eat and argue with? You say your shorter than him but it's not clear how tall

he is. Is the movie star you're cavorting with taller than him?

4   Did you actually adopt a cat, despite everyone knowing how allergic you are? Is it's hair short? Shorter than Charles'?

5   The project your working on—what's its title? And whom, may I ask, is your assistant? If you and your assistant's efforts pay off, will you take all the credit for yourself?

6   Finally, what are Charles' feelings about hummus? The chapter leaves my fellow readers and I in the dark.

7   I will very much appreciate you answering my questions.

Ms. Led

P.S. I think your running for office is a good idea. You won't have to wonder whom to vote for.

ANSWERS TO CASE QUIZ

- Paragraph 1 is correct, except for *between you and I* in the second sentence. That should read *between you and me* because it's a phrase, and phrases don't contain subjects (the pronoun *I* is a subject; the pronoun *me* is an object).

- Paragraph 2 is correct.

- Paragraph 3 contains four errors. In the second sentence, *who* should be *whom* because this clause already has a subject (*you*). In the third sentence, *your* should be *you're* because the writer means "you are"; *him* should be *he* because the writer means "shorter than he is." In the fourth sentence, *him* should be *he* because the writer means "taller than he is."

- Paragraph 4 contains two errors. In the first sentence, *everyone knowing* should be *everyone's knowing* because the writer is speaking about everyone's action (*knowing* is a gerund requiring a possessive word before it). In the second sentence, *it's* should be *its* because the writer needs the possessive form of *it*, not the contraction for *it is*.

- Paragraph 5 contains two errors for sure, and possibly three. In the first sentence, *your* should be *you're* because the writer means "you are." In the second sentence, *whom* should be *who* because the upcoming verb (*is*) needs a subject. The third sentence can be considered correct if the meaning is "the efforts belong jointly to you and your assistant." But if the writer means "you and your assistant own separate efforts," then *you* should be *your*.

- Paragraph 6 contains one error. In the second sentence, *I* should be *me*. After the verb *leaves*, you need an object, not a subject (the subject of *leaves* is *chapter*). If you delete *my fellow readers* for a moment, you'll hear the mistake: *the chapter leaves . . . I in the dark*.

- Paragraph 7 contains one error. Instead of *you answering*, it should read *your answering* because *answering* is a gerund requiring a possessive word to the left. The writer is talking about appreciating the reader's action.

- The P.S. contains no error.

Chapter 2: Agreement

Agreement is a concept that applies, first of all, to subjects and verbs: a singular subject must be followed by a singular verb form; a plural subject must be followed by a plural verb form. The only time you have to think about singular and plural verb forms is when you're using present tense; verbs in other tenses do not change form, regardless of their subjects.

Agreement also pertains to nouns and pronouns: a singular pronoun must refer to a singular noun; a plural pronoun must refer to a plural noun.

That all sounds pretty reasonable, doesn't it? Singular goes with singular; plural goes with plural. Yet it's not always easy to diagnose the situation.

Subject-Verb Agreement

Subjects vs. other nouns

When a subject and verb are not far away from one another, it's easy to choose the right verb form. For example,

> *Cash purchases are valid.*

> *Cash purchases made in June are valid.*

> *Cash purchases made in June or July of this year are valid.*

The verb in each of those sentences (***are***) is plural because the subject in each of those sentences (***purchases***) is plural. Even though the verb drifts farther away from the subject in each sample sentence, the subject remains memorable and the correct verb form is therefore easy to select. Now, consider another sentence:

> *Only purchases made by an end-user customer or commercial business from an authorized HP reseller in the United States and U.S. territories are valid.*

By the time you reach the twenty-third word of that sentence, you can easily forget what the subject is. You've met so many nouns—***purchases, customer, business, reseller, United States, territories***—that it's hard to know what to choose for a verb. Do you end with ***is valid*** (singular) or ***are valid*** (plural)? The answer depends on which of those nouns is the subject. You can find the subject by asking "Who or what is valid?" The answer, **purchases**, tells you that **are valid** (plural verb form) is correct.

Vague subjects

Another type of subject that can be difficult to diagnose is a vague word—like **any**, **either**, **neither**, or **none**—followed by a prepositional phrase. Here are some examples:

> *Any of these products falls within your budget.*

> *Either of these products meets your software needs.*

> *Neither of these products is going to solve your marital difficulties.*

> *None of these products comes with a warranty.*

As you may already understand from the singular verb forms in those sentences, the vague words that begin the sentences are singular. And they are subjects. What about the word **products**? Why isn't **products** a subject? Because it follows a preposition (**of**), and no word that follows a preposition is a subject.

It may be easier to remember that **any**, **either**, and **neither** are singular if you realize that they stand for **any one**, **either one**, and **neither one**. Here are the first three sample sentences again, with the word **one** included:

Any one of these products falls within your budget.

Either one of these products meets your software needs.

Neither one of these products is going to solve your marital difficulties.

How about the word **none**? You can remember that it's singular by considering it a contraction for **not one**. In other words,

None (not one) of these products comes with a warranty.

Speaking of **one**, what's the difference between **anyone** and **any one**? Or between **everyone** and **every one**? First, they are all grammatically singular, regardless of meaning. But there is a difference in meaning between the one- and two-word versions: when you type **anyone** or **everyone**, you're referring to people; when you type **any one** or **every one**, you may be referring to people, but not necessarily—it depends on what follows or what is understood. For example, perhaps you mean "any one of the customers" or "every one of the customers" (in which case you are referring to people); or maybe you mean "any one of the petunias" or "every one of the petunias" (in which case you are not referring to people). In sum, **any one** and **every one** mean one of a group (of people or things), rather than one person (**anyone**) or a bunch of people (**everyone**).

Unusual noun forms

Some nouns in our language are spelled in an unfamiliar way (because they are Latin) and therefore lead to agreement errors. *Criteria*, *media*, and *data*, for instance, are plural. Therefore, when they serve as subjects, any present-tense verb that follows must also be plural. The following sentences are correct:

> *The criteria are not impossible to meet.*
>
> *The media swarm over a scandal.*
>
> *The data seem easy to interpret.*

If you want the singular form of *criteria*, use *criterion*.
If you want the singular form of *media*, use *medium*.
If you want the singular form of *data*, find another way to say it (the singular of *data* is *datum*, but it's rarely used).

Mass nouns

Also related to agreement are the nouns in our language that do not have a plural form, even though they may refer to a group of elements. These are nouns like *advice*, *equipment*, *furniture*, and *jewelry*. They are called mass nouns, and they never end in the letter *s*. They are grammatically singular, which means that when they serve as subjects, the upcoming verb must be singular. A list of common mass nouns appears at the end of this chapter (page 29).

Two nouns in subject position

When do two singular nouns become a plural subject? Only when they are joined by **and**. Here is an example:

> *Che and Fidel are about to start a revolution.*

There are several words that sound equivalent to **and** but they do not have the power to join two singular nouns into a double subject. These include **as well as**, **along with**, **together with**, and **plus**. When two singular nouns are connected by any of these words, the result is a singular subject.

Consider the following sentences:

> *Che, as well as Fidel, believes in equal opportunity for all.*

> *Che, along with Fidel, has captured the hearts of his countrymen.*

> *Che, together with Fidel, gratefully acknowledges his loyal following.*

> *Che, plus Fidel, never shows up without a cigar.*

What happens when two singular nouns are joined by **or**? The result is a singular subject because now you're talking about one noun or the other noun, not both:

> *Che or Fidel is the one to ask about socialism.*

The same is true of two subjects joined by *either . . . or* or *neither . . . nor*:

> *Either Che or Fidel is supposed to sign autographs at the rally.*

> *Neither Che nor Fidel has a pen.*

If a singular and a plural noun, joined by *and*, appear at the beginning of a sentence, place the singular noun first and make the verb plural. For example,

> *Fidel and his cigars have become famous throughout the world.*

Noun-Pronoun Agreement

It's common sense that you need a singular pronoun to refer to a singular noun and you need a plural pronoun to refer to a plural noun. Everyone knows that. But not everyone remembers the noun when it comes time to choose a pronoun. Or a person may remember the noun but doesn't want to burden his/her sentence with a double pronoun (like *his/her*). Or the noun in question looks singular but represents many. So errors in noun-pronoun agreement crop up.

Clear nouns → hazy memories

Sometimes a faulty pronoun reference occurs simply because someone doesn't remember the noun she wrote or remembers it inaccurately (she assumes it's plural when, in fact, it's singular, or vice versa). The resulting error looks pretty bad:

> *Fidel signed the <u>papers</u> and then buried <u>it</u> under a mango tree.*

♀ The solution is to match the pronoun to the noun:

> *Fidel signed the <u>papers</u> and then buried <u>them</u> under a mango tree.*

Singular generic words → avoidance of double pronouns

A faulty pronoun reference can also occur when someone doesn't want to use a double pronoun reference (*he/she, him/her, his/her*) even though the generic word it refers to is singular:

> *<u>Anyone</u> can find those papers if <u>they</u> have a bloodhound and a shovel.*

♀ There are three ways to fix this error.

• You can use **he/she**, if you need it only once (it becomes awkward when repeated):

> *<u>Anyone</u> can find those papers if <u>he/she</u> has a bloodhound and a shovel.*

• You can use **he** or **she** by itself, as long as you use the alternative pronoun somewhere else in your document:

> *Anyone can find those papers if he has a bloodhound
> and a shovel.*

- You can change the singular generic word to a plural
  word and then keep your plural pronoun:

> *People can find those papers if they have a bloodhound
> and a shovel.*

Singular nouns representing groups → distracted focus

A faulty pronoun reference can result from focusing on
the meaning of a noun rather than on its singular form.
Many nouns (*committee, jury, company, firm, team, university*) are singular while representing many components. Rather than recognizing and dealing with this
discrepancy, people often leave the noun in singular form
and follow it with a plural pronoun:

> *The new government wanted to see the papers Fidel had
> signed, but they never thought to dig under a mango tree
> to find them.*

♀ There are two ways to fix this inconsistency.

- If you need to keep the plural pronoun ***they*** because
  the singular pronoun ***it*** sounds illogical (***it never
  thought to dig under a mango tree***, for example), then
  find a way to make the noun plural:

The new government officials wanted to see the papers
Fidel had signed, but they never thought to dig under a
mango tree to find them.

• If a singular pronoun sounds fine because the noun is
acting as one unified entity, then leave the noun singular and change the pronoun to *it*:

The new government wanted to see the papers Fidel had
signed, but it didn't pursue the matter.

Achieving agreement, whether between subjects and
verbs or nouns and pronouns, is a matter of remembering what's already on the page while continuing to write.
People tend to focus exclusively on the word they're
about to type, rather than bearing in mind the words they
already typed.

Forgetting what happened earlier in a sentence can result
not only in agreement errors but also in illogical statements. Take a look at the following sentence.

People riding bicycles, instead of driving cars,
is good for their health as well as their
environment.

When reduced to its basic components (subject, verb, and
key words that complete the meaning), that sentence says,
"People . . . is good for health and environment." What the

author meant to convey, of course, is that riding bicycles is good for health and environment. If the writer had kept in mind what she wrote at the beginning of the sentence (**People**), she wouldn't have continued with *is*; she would have chosen *are*. And, with **People are** clearly in mind, she wouldn't have completed her sentence with **good for their health as well as their environment**; she would have apprehended the nonsense before it hit the page.

In a case like this—when the balance of a sentence contains the right message, but it makes no sense with the subject—the best remedy is to change the subject:

> *Riding bicycles, instead of driving cars, is good for people's health as well as their environment.*

To ensure both agreement and logic in all of your sentences, think of your words as musical notes. They may be clear and beautiful on their own, but are they in harmony with the others? Keep your ears open.

Common Mass Nouns

(no *s* on the end)

admiration	feedback	jargon	public
advice	fitness	jealousy	punctuation
aggravation	flattery	jewelry	rage
anger	furniture	justice	recovery
anticipation	garbage	knowledge	reliance
appreciation	gossip	literacy	respect
assistance	grammar	litigation	revenge
awareness	gratitude	logic	reverence
baggage	hardware	luck	shame
bravery	hate	luggage	sheep
cash	health	mail	slang
compliance	heat	management	software
comprehension	help	manipulation	stamina
concentration	hesitation	merchandise	starvation
confusion	homework	morale	stimulation
consciousness	honesty	nonsense	stuff
consideration	honor	offspring	support
correspondence	hospitality	oppression	training
darkness	hostility	optimism	trash
devotion	humanity	participation	understanding
diligence	humility	pay	valor
empathy	illiteracy	perseverance	vehemence
energy	imagination	pessimism	violence
entertainment	immorality	police	warmth
enthusiasm	implementation	pride	waste
envy	independence	privacy	weather
equality	information	proof	
equipment	integrity	propaganda	
evidence	intimidation	prudence	

QUIZ ON AGREEMENT

Below is a letter to Che from Fidel. Your job is to edit the letter for agreement. That is, look at all the present-tense verbs to see whether they agree with their subjects, and inspect all pronouns to see whether they agree with the nouns they're referring to. If the sentence is correct, leave it alone; if it's not, fix it.

Dear Che:

1   I want you to know how excited and optimistic I am about the revolution we are planning. For a long time I have wanted to change things in this country so that all the people—regardless of race, creed, or smoking habit—has equal access to health care, education, and cigars. (I have also longed for a sizeable audience to listen to my speeches. My family hear my ideas, but there's only eight of them and they walk away after five minutes. I want a large group that stay transfixed for hours.)

2   Now, we need to think about practical matters. For example, who will run the military, once we take over? My brothers are interested, but none of them have a neat appearance. We need someone who at least shines their shoes.

3   And what about the economy? If we shut down the casinos, where will the money come from? Producing enough sugar and tobacco to satisfy our people and to export abroad are extremely important.

4   Public opinion is important, too. We want to create a good image to ensure that the media presents us in a positive light. If another country thinks we have a worthy cause, they may consider lending a helping hand. Speaking of hands, we'll need to shake many in the near future, which pose a health risk. Maybe we should stick to passing out cigars.

5   So much to think about, eh? Let me know your feedbacks soon.

Fidel

ANSWERS TO AGREEMENT QUIZ

- Paragraph 1 contains four errors. In the second sentence, the verb *has* should be *have*, to agree with its plural subject *all the people*. In the fourth sentence, the subject *family* should be reworded as plural (*family members*, for instance) so that the upcoming plural verb (*hear*) agrees; also in this sentence, *there's* should be *there are*, to agree with *eight*. In the fifth sentence, *stay* should be *stays*, to agree with its singular subject *group*.

- Paragraph 2 contains two errors. In the third sentence, the verb *have* should be *has*, to agree with the singular subject *none*. In the fourth sentence, the pronoun *their* should be *his*, to agree with the singular word *someone*.

- Paragraph 3 contains one error. In the third sentence, the verb *are* should be *is*, to agree with its singular subject *Producing*.

- Paragraph 4 contains three errors. In the second sentence, the verb *presents* should be *present*, to agree with its plural subject *media*. In the third sentence, the pronoun *they* should be *it*, to agree with the singular noun *country*. In the fourth sentence, the verb *pose* should be *poses* because its subject, *which*, refers to the action of shaking hands (that action poses a health risk).

- Paragraph 5 contains one error. There should be no *s* on *feedback*. That noun is always singular.

Chapter 3: Verb Tense and Usage

Tense refers to the different forms that verbs assume, to indicate the time zone of an action. Although there are many tenses in English (past, present, future, past perfect, present perfect, future perfect, and the continuous form of each of those six), only a few contexts typically cause problems.

Present

It's easy to choose present tense when the action is physically happening at the moment (*Natasha is waltzing down the hallway*) or when it occurs often (*Natasha waltzes down the hallway every morning*). It's not so easy to choose present tense when you're discussing a text you finished reading, a film you saw, or a conversation you had. Take a look at the following sentences:

> *The article indicated that Natasha has been dancing since she was born.*

> *Natasha showed me a videotape that proved the article right.*

> *Natasha said that she still loved to dance.*

In the first sentence, **indicated** should be **indicates**. Whenever the subject is any kind of text—*article*, *book*, *chapter*, *memo*, *letter*, *report*, *e-mail*, *passage*, *paragraph*, *sentence*, *phrase*—the verb should be present tense, since the text still exists. Even though you read it in the past, it is still conveying the information you're referring to.

In the second sentence, **proved** should be **proves**. Even though Natasha showed me a videotape in the past, that tape is still proving the article right.

In the third sentence, **loved** should be **loves**. What Natasha said, in the past, is that she still loves to dance, in the present. You need to separate the time zone in which the person spoke from the time zone that the person spoke about. The two are not always the same.

Here are the previous sample sentences in correct form:

> *The article indicates that Natasha has been dancing since she was born.*

> *Natasha showed me a videotape that proves the article right.*

> *Natasha said that she still loves to dance.*

Present Perfect

This tense involves **have** or **has** as a helping verb, plus a past participle (*asked*, *danced*). It represents action that began in the past, continued over time, and extends to the present moment. For example,

> *I have often asked Natasha how old she is.*

> *She has danced around the question more than once.*

Have asked and **has danced** are correct because those verbs represent past action that happened intermittently between a past moment and the present moment.

The problem with present perfect is not that people don't use it when they should; it's that people use it when they shouldn't. Specifically, they use it when they should be using simple past tense, to refer to a completed past action that happened once. Here are some examples of the typical mistake:

> *I have received Natasha's most recent letter, in which she has described the proper way to do the two-step. I have decided to read it when I have more energy.*

Three verbs in that paragraph (**have received**, **has described**, and **have decided**) should be simple past tense (**received**, **described**, and **decided**) because they refer to completed past actions that happened once.

Past Perfect

This tense involves **had** as a helping verb, followed by a past participle (*asked, danced*). It represents a past action that happened earlier than a nearby past action. In other words, when you are writing about something that occurred in the simple past, and you also refer to something that occurred <u>before</u> that point, you need past-perfect tense. The following sentences are correct:

> *Natasha said that she had applied for a dance scholarship to kindergarten.*

> *She did not receive a scholarship because she had not revealed her true age on the application.*

> *She had claimed that she was five when, in fact, she was thirteen.*

> *Her parents had kept her out of school until she could manage to sit still.*

Do all those tenses make sense to you? In the first sentence, **had applied** is correct because that action happened before **said**. In the second sentence, **had not revealed** is correct because that action happened before **did not receive**. In the third sentence, **had claimed** is correct because that action took place at the same time as **had not revealed** (in the previous sentence). And in the fourth sentence, **had kept** is correct because that action happened before **could manage**.

The problem with past perfect is that people don't use it when they should. Instead, they express chronological past actions in the same tense, as if they had all happened at the same time. Here are the four sample sentences again, with all verbs in simple past tense:

> *Natasha said that she applied for a dance scholarship to kindergarten.*

> *She did not receive a scholarship because she did not reveal her true age on the application.*

> *She claimed that she was five when, in fact, she was thirteen.*

> *Her parents kept her out of school until she could manage to sit still.*

If those sentences sound fine to you, that's because you are used to hearing the error. "If the mistake sounds right," you may ask, "why do I need to avoid it?" Because there are times when the error can lead to misunderstanding. For example,

> *Natasha said that she felt cheated.*

That sentence means that Natasha felt cheated at the same moment that she said it. If she means that she felt cheated when she was in kindergarten, then the second verb should be past perfect:

> *Natasha said that she had felt cheated.*

Confusing Verbs

In this category are some irregular verbs, some regular verbs with irregular requirements, and some verbs that people just don't spell right.

Troublesome irregular verbs

A verb is called regular when it takes **ed** on the end to become past tense or a past participle. For example,

> *Yesterday Natasha beamed as she was cheered by the crowd.*

> *She was thrilled because she had finally graduated from elementary school.*

A verb is called irregular when it takes an ending other than **ed** to become past tense or a past participle. People handle most irregular verbs correctly without batting an eyelid. For example, they automatically turn **think** into **thought** and **sink** into **sank**. But when it comes to **lie** and **lay**, people rarely get it right.

Lie, as in **to lie down**, is conjugated like this:

> **lie**

> **lay**

> **lain**

In other words,

> *Today Natasha lies on the couch; yesterday she lay on the couch; and before that she had lain on the couch.*

Lay, as in **to lay an egg**, is conjugated like this:

> **lay**
>
> **laid**
>
> **laid**

In other words,

> *Today Natasha lays her dancing shoes to rest; yesterday she laid them to rest; and before that she had laid them to rest.*

Besides the different ways in which **lie** and **lay** are conjugated, there's a grammatical difference: **lie** cannot be followed immediately by any noun or pronoun; **lay** must be followed immediately by a noun or pronoun. We do not **lie** something down; we **lay** something down. We do not **lay** down (not in present tense, anyway); we **lie** down.

How can you remember this? If you're referring to putting your own body on a couch or a bed, you need **lie**, **lay**, **lain**. If you're referring to putting another entity somewhere, you need **lay**, **laid**, **laid**.

Thoroughly confused? Lay this book aside and lie down for a while.

Another verb that people don't handle very well is **drink**. Here's how it's conjugated:

> **drink**
>
> **drank**
>
> **drunk**

In other words,

> *Today Natasha drinks tea; yesterday she drank tea; before that she had drunk tea; and, in fact, she has drunk gallons of tea this week.*

People tend to avoid using **drunk** where it belongs. They write, for example, "I have drank a lot of water today." Perhaps they don't use **drunk** because they associate the word with too much alcohol. **Drunk** refers to alcohol when it shows up after **am**, **is**, **are**, **was**, **were**, etc. But after **has** or **have**, **drunk** simply indicates the time zone in which any drinking action took place.

Maybe because people avoid **drunk**, they also shy away from **shrunk**. They write, for example, "Even before the commercial announcement, the audience had shrank significantly." That audience had not shrank; it had shrunk.

Regular verbs with irregular requirements

After verbs like ***request***, ***recommend***, ***suggest***, or ***demand***, you must use a noun, gerund, or noun clause (a clause beginning with ***that***). For example,

> *Natasha requested <u>a diploma</u> from her elementary school.*

> *I recommend <u>giving</u> her that diploma.*

> *Her mother demands <u>that the diploma be issued</u> with honors.*

Mistakes tend to happen after ***recommend***, in particular. The error typically looks like this:

> *I recommend you to apply for your diploma.*

That sentence is wrong because the author is not recommending a person; he is recommending an action. So the sentence should look like this:

> *I recommend <u>applying</u> for your diploma.*

or

> *I recommend <u>that you apply</u> for your diploma.*

Don't think that ***recommend someone*** is always wrong. You <u>can</u> recommend someone—<u>for</u> something (a job, a role, an honor, an award); you just can't recommend someone <u>to do something</u>.

Frequently misspelled verbs

recur   When something occurs again, it
                 <u>recurs</u> (not reoccurs).

lose   When something slips away from you,
                 you <u>lose</u> it (not loose it; *loose* is the
                 opposite of *tight*).

ensure   When you want to make sure that
                 something happens, you want to
                 <u>ensure</u> (not insure) that it takes place.

assure   When you want to comfort people,
                 you <u>assure</u> them that everything will
                 be all right.

insure   When you want to ensure that you'll
                 be reimbursed for lost property (and
                 assure yourself that you'll be able to
                 buy it again), you <u>insure</u> your belong-
                 ings. *Insure* relates to insurance.

affect   When you're writing about how some-
                 thing will influence the situation,
                 you're referring to how it will <u>affect</u>
                 the situation (not effect; *effect* is a
                 noun meaning "consequence" or
                 "outcome").

let's   If you mean to say "let us" (as in *let us be honest*), type **let's**, not **lets**. **Let's** is a contraction for **let us**. **Lets** is a verb (meaning "allows/permits") that needs a subject to the left of it, as in *Natasha lets the dog in when she needs a dancing partner.*

accommodate   This word contains two **c**'s and two **m**'s (not one **m**).

Here are four more verbs that are often misrepresented:

imply   When your words contain an underlying message, you are implying something.

infer   When you detect an underlying message in someone else's words, you are inferring something.

lend   When you allow someone to borrow something, you lend it (not loan it; **loan** is a noun that refers to what you lent).

try to   When you attempt to do something, you try to do it (not try and do it).

Verbs are the very hearts of your sentences, pumping life into an otherwise inert body of people, places, things, descriptions, and glue. Because verbs are so critical to the vitality of your writing, you need to select them with care and monitor them closely.

Monitor them for what?

- As you learned from the previous chapter, verbs must agree with their subjects (in terms of number) and make sense with the words around them.

- As you learned from this chapter, verbs must reflect the appropriate time zone, standard usage, and dictionary spelling.

Is that all? Almost. The next chapter explains the last issue you need to understand to form all of your verbs correctly.

QUIZ ON TENSE AND USAGE

Below is a letter to Natasha from her elementary school. Your job is to edit the letter for tense only. That is, look at all verbs to see whether they are correct in terms of time zone and usage. If the sentence is correct, leave it alone; if it's not, fix it.

Dear Natasha:

1   We have recently received your request for a diploma from our elementary school. Given the amount of time that has elapsed, we wondered why we didn't hear from you sooner. In response to your inquiry, we have carefully reviewed your records.

2   Your report cards indicated that while you attended our school, you performed extremely well in math problems involving numbers one through four. You had trouble dealing with numbers five through nine

because, as you once told your teacher, no dance step involved counting beyond four.

3   Your performance in English seemed to be satisfactory. Although you read superficially, leaping over much of the text, you were on your toes during exams.

4   P.E. was another story. Let's just say that your behavior was unusual. For example, during softball practice you pirouetted in the outfield, made yourself dizzy, and never caught a ball. Furthermore, you laid down and fanned yourself frequently. When an inning was over, you bowed to the empty bleachers and waited around for a bouquet.

5   It's fortunate that we didn't loose your records. Documentation ensures us that you did attend a graduation ceremony. But there was no evidence of any diploma.

6   We have decided to consult with the district superintendent on this matter. If she recommends us to issue you a diploma at this late date, we will gladly do so.

Your old principal

ANSWERS TO TENSE AND USAGE QUIZ

- Paragraph 1 contains three errors. In the first sentence, *have received* should be *received*. *Received* is a completed past action that happened once, calling for simple past tense. In the second sentence, *didn't hear* should be *hadn't heard* because this action happened before *wondered*; or *wondered* should be *wonder*, which will make sense with *didn't hear*. (The question here is whether the school officials wondered in the past or are wondering now.) In the third sentence, *have reviewed* should be *reviewed* because the reviewing action is complete. (Even though it happened over time, it doesn't extend to the present moment.)

- Paragraph 2 contains two errors. In the first sentence, the verb *indicated* should be *indicate*. Present tense is in order because the subject of this verb is *report cards*—written documents that still exist and still indicate something. At the end of the second sentence, the verb *involved* should be *involves* because what Natasha told her teacher is still true—that no dance step involves counting beyond four.

- Paragraph 3 contains one error. In the first sentence, **seemed** should be **seems** because Natasha's performance of many years ago presently seems satisfactory to the author of the letter. (If the author were talking about how Natasha's teachers viewed her performance in the past, then **seemed** would be correct.)

- Paragraph 4 contains three errors. In the first sentence, **was** should be **is** because the story that the author refers to still exists. (The opening sentences of paragraphs 2, 3, and 4 are alike in that each tells what the author presently concludes.) In the second sentence, **Lets** should be **Let's** because the author means "let us." In the fourth sentence, **laid** should be **lay** because the author needs the past tense of **lie**.

- Paragraph 5 contains three errors. In the first sentence, **loose** should be **lose**. In the second sentence, **ensures** should be **assures**. In the third sentence, **was** should be **is** because the author is talking about evidence that still doesn't exist.

- Paragraph 6 contains two errors. In the first sentence, **have decided** should be **decided**. **Decided** is a completed past action that happened once, not something that happened over time and extends to the present. In the second sentence, **us to issue** should be **issuing** or **that we issue** (the verb **recommends** must be followed by a noun, gerund, or noun clause).

Chapter 4: Verb Mood

Like **_tense_**, **_mood_** refers to verb form. Instead of indicating the time zone of an action, however, the mood of a verb tells whether the action is real or not.

Indicative Mood

If you're writing an action that did occur, is occurring, or will occur, you're using indicative mood.

Examples:

> _Rover <u>entered</u> the room as soon as I <u>turned</u> on the TV._
>
> _He <u>is lying</u> on the couch, hoping to watch_ Animal Cops.
>
> _I <u>will ask</u> him to move over so that I <u>can have</u> a seat._

Imperative Mood

If you're writing an action that commands the reader to do something, you're using imperative mood.

Examples:

> *<u>Move</u> over, Rover.*
>
> *Please <u>don't</u> take up the whole couch.*
>
> *And <u>stop</u> chewing on the remote control.*

Subjunctive Mood

If you're writing an action that isn't happening or isn't true, yet the sentence speculates about it, you're using subjunctive mood.

Examples:

> *Rover yawned when I asked him to move over, as if I <u>had</u> <u>been talking</u> about the weather.*
>
> *If Rover <u>had</u> any manners, he <u>would make</u> room for me on the couch.*
>
> *I wish Rover <u>were</u> more considerate.*

Indicative and imperative moods don't cause problems; people handle them correctly without thinking. Subjunctive mood, however, is challenging. Special verb forms are necessary when you're speculating about actions that aren't happening or aren't true—i.e., when you're making hypothetical points, projecting what could have been or what would be. There are several contexts that require subjunctive mood, as well as a few different ways to express it. What follows is a discussion of some key words that should put you on subjunctive alert.

As if and as though

Whenever you're using **as if** or **as though**, you're at the beginning of a clause that may or may not require subjunctive mood. How you treat the verb in that clause depends on what you want to convey—that an action is true or possible, or that an action isn't true or possible.

If you mean that something is true or possible, you don't need to use subjunctive mood—you choose normal verb forms that depict the time zone you're talking about.

Examples:

> *Rover bounded into the room as if he <u>expected</u> a treat.*

> *He chews on the remote control as though he <u>is</u> hungry.*

In those sentences, the verbs that follow *as if* and *as though* are what I'm calling normal—they are past tense for a past moment and present tense for a present moment, to convey that the actions are possibly true. (In the first example, it is possible that Rover expected a treat when he bounded into the room; in the second example, it is possible that he is hungry as he chews on the remote control.)

When, on the other hand, you want to indicate that an action is not true or possible, you need to apply a special treatment to the verb that follows *as if* or *as though*. Specifically, you need to use past-tense verb forms that don't literally depict the time zones you're talking about.

Examples:

> *Rover monopolizes the couch as if it were his property.*

> *He acts as though he had purchased it with his hard-won allowance.*

In the first example, the verb following *as if* is simple past tense, to convey that a point about the present is not true.

In the second example, the verb following *as though* is past-perfect tense, to convey that a point about the past did not happen.

Do you see the pattern? To communicate that an action isn't true or happening, you step one rung down the tense ladder: for a point about the present, use past tense; for a point about the past, use past-perfect tense.

"Yes," you may say, "but why does the first example contain *were* when the subject is *it*? Shouldn't it be 'as if it was his property?'" No, it shouldn't—not when you're talking about an action that isn't presently true or happening. If you need a verb that comes from *to be*, choose *were*, no matter what the subject is.

More examples:

> *I choose to watch* Judge Judy, *as if Rover were interested in it.*

> *Rover looks at me as though I were nuts.*

In those **as if** and **as though** clauses, the subject changes (from **Rover** to **I**), but the verb remains **were**.

When people need the past tense of other verbs, they have no problem because they have no choice: every verb, except **to be**, has only one form of simple past tense. Only **to be** has two—**was** and **were**. That's why people get confused. They know to use past tense; they don't know to use **were**.

Here are the previous sample sentences again, this time containing the prevalent **was** mistake:

I choose to watch Judge Judy, *as if Rover was interested in it.*

Rover looks at me as though I was nuts.

If I mean to convey that Rover is not interested in *Judge Judy* and that I am not nuts, then I need to use **were** to show that what I am speculating about isn't true.

If

When you're using **if** to speculate about a situation that is possible, you automatically use normal verb tenses throughout the sentence (past, present, or future, depending on the time zone you're discussing).

Examples:

If Rover already watched Animal Cops *earlier in the day, he may let me see a bit of* Judge Judy *now.*

If Rover insists on watching Animal Cops *now, I will have to give in.*

If I don't give in, I will be in the dog house.

When you're using **if** to speculate about a situation that is not possible, you need to use subjunctive mood throughout the sentence—in the clause that starts with **if** and in the other clause as well. (In this regard, sentences involving *if* are different from those involving *as if* or *as though*: in sentences containing *if*, both clauses are speculating about something; in sentences containing *as if* or *as though*, only one clause is speculating.)

Here are some examples of present subjunctive mood inside sentences involving *if*:

> If Rover really cared about me, he would let me watch Judge Judy.

> I would ignore Rover's program preference, if he weren't so big.

> If I got into a fight with Rover, he would surely win.

Note that all the verbs in those sentences are past tense, to convey a present situation that isn't true or happening.

Here are some examples of past subjunctive mood inside sentences involving *if*:

> If I had known about Rover's penchant for Animal Cops, I would never have bought a TV.

> I would not have bought the TV anyway if it hadn't been on sale.

> If Rover had had his way, I would have purchased two TVs.

Note that the verbs inside those sentences are in more complicated forms of past tense, to convey a past situation that wasn't true or happening. The verbs inside the *if* clauses all contain **had** plus a past participle.[1] The verbs inside the independent clauses start with **would have** and end in a past participle. That's how we communicate that a past action we're speculating about did not take place.

In sentences like these, **would** always means that what you're talking about is not true, not happening, or not likely.[2] You need to watch your use of **would** so that it doesn't sneak into sentences that otherwise convey possibility. Look at the following mixed messages:

> If I get rid of the TV, I would have to get rid of Rover.

> I would be miserable if I have no one to argue with.

Those sentences represent a common error: implying possibility in one clause and impossibility in the other. You can't do that. You need to decide what you want to communicate—that something is possible or not—and then make your verbs consistent throughout the sentence. Here are some ways to revise the previous sample sentences:

> If I get rid of the TV, I will have to get rid of Rover.
> (possible—may happen)

> If I got rid of the TV, I would have to get rid of Rover.
> (impossible—not going to happen)

---

[1] In the third example, **had had** may look strange, but it's correct. **Had had** occurs when the helping verb is **had** and the participle comes from **to have**.

[2] **Could** also implies improbability. **Can** is the alternative that says an action is possible.

I will be miserable if I have no one to argue with.
(possible—may happen)

I would be miserable if I had no one to argue with.
(impossible—not going to happen)

Wish

Whenever you use **wish** (as a verb, not a noun), you need subjunctive mood in the clause(s) that follow.[3] The verb **wish,** by definition, introduces actions that are not presently true and not likely to happen.

Examples:

I wish that Rover were a Pomeranian so that there would be room for me on the couch.

I wish that Animal Cops were aired only in Switzerland.

Rover wishes that I were better trained.

Again, the verb **were** follows **Rover, Animal Cops,** and **I** because those clauses express present impossibilities (that Rover is a Pomeranian, that *Animal Cops* is aired only in Switzerland, and that I am better trained). Note that **would be** occurs in the last clause of the first example, to indicate another present impossibility—that there is room for me on the couch.

---

[3] If **wish** is followed only by a pronoun and a noun, as in *I wish you luck,* you needn't think about mood.

The common error in this type of sentence is our old pal **was**:

> *I wish that Rover was a Pomeranian . . .*

> *I wish that Animal Cops was aired . . .*

> *Rover wishes that I was . . .*

Never use **was** after **wish**. It is always wrong.

If the opening clause does not contain **wish**—i.e., if the sentence depicts a past action that may have occurred—then, **was** is correct, of course.

Examples:

> *Rover hoped that I was too tired to watch TV.*

> *He looked as if he was sure I'd give up on Judge Judy.*

> *If he was nervous, he wasn't showing it.*

Feeling overwhelmed by the **was/were** challenge? Here's a reminder to lighten your mood: no other verb in our language has two forms of simple past tense. What if you had to think twice about every verb that follows **as if**, **as though**, **if**, and **wish**? Would you move to Switzerland (where they have three languages and no *Animal Cops*)?

QUIZ ON MOOD

Below is a letter from Rover to his owner. Your job is to edit the letter for mood. That is, look at all the verbs to see what they imply: that the action is true/possible or untrue/impossible. If the verb form conveys the right message, leave it alone; if it doesn't, fix it.

Dear Owner:

1   When I selected you as an adoptive guardian, I had no idea what I was getting myself into. You looked clean, you smelled good, you didn't bark or growl. You acted as if you've been around the block a few times.

2   After living with you for three months, I can see that you need a few pointers. For example, do you think it's polite to stand around glaring at me while I watch

TV? Why don't you sit on the floor, like a good girl, and just look at the images? Even if you don't understand the story, you can act as though you did.

3   Also, being a dog's best friend doesn't mean that you have to sit right next to me on the couch. What do you think they make rugs for? Obviously, we don't need them for walking. And, if there were a tree or fire hydrant around, we don't need them when nature calls, either. So they must be for sitting.

4   Let me clarify something: rugs are for sitting if the sitter has a little meat on her bones. Someone like you, for example, with built-in padding, wouldn't need more than a thin rug under her. Someone in leaner shape—like me, for instance—would need a cushion or two. If you insist on sharing the couch, you'd need to buy a bigger one.

5   Finally, I wish I was free to enjoy my favorite program without all that grumbling you do. If you want to watch a different show, you could always get another TV.

6   I think our next walk should be to an electronics store. You can sit outside and wait patiently for me while I shop.

Rover

ANSWERS TO MOOD QUIZ

- Paragraph 1 contains one error. In the third sentence, **'ve** (short for **have**) should be **'d** (short for **had**), since Rover is talking about a past action that didn't happen—that is, his owner had not been around the block a few times.

- Paragraph 2 contains no error. The final verb in the fourth sentence (**did**) is the one in question, since it occurs after **as though**. **Did** is correct because the sentence already set the condition **even if you don't understand . . .** , so the final clause refers to something that isn't true (**as though you did**).

- Paragraph 3 contains one error. In the fourth sentence, **were** should be **is** because Rover means to convey the possibility that a tree or fire hydrant is around. (The verb in the next clause, **don't need**, correctly conveys possibility.)

- Paragraph 4 contains three errors. In the second sentence, **wouldn't need** should be **doesn't need** because

Rover is stating what he believes to be true. For the same reason, in the third sentence, **would need** should be **needs**. In the last sentence, the verb in the second clause, **'d need**, should be **'ll need**. **'D need** is short for **would need**, which is subjunctive; the verb in the previous clause, **insist**, is indicative. Indicative is the correct mood for both clauses because Rover means to convey possibility—i.e., that if his owner insists . . . , she will need to buy . . . .

- Paragraph 5 contains two errors. In the first sentence, **was** should be **were** because it follows the verb **wish**. In the second sentence, **could** should be **can** because Rover is talking about a possibility. (The verb in the previous clause, **want**, conveys possibility; therefore, the verb in the second clause should do the same.)

- Paragraph 6 contains no error.

Chapter 5: Modifiers

Modifiers are words that describe. They come in various forms (word, phrase, clause) and they can change the shape of anything you write, defining and refining it to the degree you want.

Example, no modifier:
    David moved.

Example, a few modifiers:
    David, my dear brother, moved to Timbuktu, where he has many friends.

Example, several modifiers:
    After doing a lot of serious thinking about his life, my dear brother, David, who had lived comfortably in San Francisco for many years, recently moved to Timbuktu, a well-known word but a little-known town.

The first example doesn't tell you much because it contains only subject and verb.

The second example tells you something about *David* (he is a brother), about *brother* (this brother is dear and he belongs to me), about *moved* (where he moved), and about *Timbuktu* (he has many friends there).

The third example tells you more about *David* (he did some thinking, he is my brother, and he had lived in San Francisco); about the kind of *thinking* he did (it was a lot, it was serious, and it was about his life); about *brother* (he is dear and he is mine); about how, when, and where he *had lived* (comfortably, for many years, and in San Francisco); about when and where he *moved* (recently and to Timbuktu); about *Timbuktu* (it is a word and a town); about *word* (it is well known); and about *town* (it is little known).

Some of the modifiers in the third example are simple adjectives (words describing nouns) and adverbs (words describing verbs) that are easy to recognize and easy to handle. No one would have any difficulty, for example, with **serious thinking**, **my dear brother**, **lived comfortably**, or **recently moved**. The adjectives are one word each and they appear directly before the nouns they describe; the adverbs end in *ly* (as well-behaved adverbs do) and they appear before or after the actions they describe, sounding fine in either spot.

Other modifiers in the third example are not as easy to recognize and handle. When a modifier shows up as a compound unit, as a phrase, or as a clause, it raises issues about punctuation and placement. This chapter discusses those issues, as well as some common errors related to modifier forms.

Compound Adjectives

A compound adjective is two or more words acting as one unit to describe someone or something. The unit is hyphenated when it appears to the left of the noun it describes.

Examples:

> *well-prepared attorney*
>
> *flea-ridden blanket*
>
> *three-year-old child*
>
> *odd-numbered rooms*
>
> *paid-for vacation*
>
> *on-the-spot decision*
>
> *up-to-date report*
>
> *first-come-first-served basis*
>
> *left- and right-handed players*
>
> *first- and second-grade teachers*

Those modifiers are hyphenated because none of the descriptive words is acting on its own; it requires the other word(s) to create the intended meaning. Specifically, the first example is not referring to a "well attorney" or simply a "prepared attorney"; the second example is not referring to a "flea blanket" or a "ridden blanket"; the third example is not referring to a "three child," a "year child," or an "old child"; and so forth.

The last two examples contain hyphens after **left** and **first** because those two words will eventually hook up with **handed** and **grade**. The spaces after **left-** and **first-** tell the reader that it will take a moment before the second half of the modifier appears. If we didn't have this technique, we'd have to repeat **handed** and **grade**:

> *left-handed and right-handed players*
>
> *first-grade and second-grade teachers*

The repetition isn't wrong, but it's clunky. Why repeat when you don't have to?

Now you know to hyphenate when descriptive words to the <u>left</u> of a noun depend on each other for meaning. What if the same descriptive words appear to the <u>right</u> of a noun? In that case, don't hyphenate.

Examples:

> *The attorney is well prepared.*
>
> *The child is three years old.*
>
> *The vacation is paid for.*

The decision was made on the spot.

The report is up to date.

The basis is first come, first served.

Once you understand this concept, the only word that can trip you up is an adverb ending in *ly*. If the first word in a string of modifiers is one of those *ly* tricksters, do not hyphenate.

Examples:

highly regarded staff

quickly written document

hastily planned vacation

minimally achieved success

lightly tossed salad

rarely used word

barely audible voice

slowly cooked rice

significantly higher rates

Adjective Phrases

A phrase (a group of words with no subject and verb) serves as an adjective when it describes somebody or something. There are two kinds of phrases that provide this service: prepositional and verbal. Most prepositional phrases don't create a problem; the only ones that pose a challenge are those beginning with **as**. Verbal phrases, however, are widely mishandled because people don't know what they are.

Phrases beginning with *as*

When a phrase begins with the preposition **as** (meaning "in the capacity of"), that phrase is describing someone or something—i.e., it is doing the job of an adjective. Therefore, it must be placed <u>next to</u> whatever it's describing.

Examples:

> *As a world traveler, David will easily adapt to a new environment.*

> *His Timbuktu friends fear that David, as a newcomer to their city, won't understand their customs.*

In both examples, the **as** phrase is placed next to **David**, the person it describes. It doesn't matter whether **David** appears before or after the phrase, as long as he's next to it. The common error occurs when people do not realize that an **as** phrase is an adjective and they place it next to the wrong noun or pronoun.

Examples:

> *As a world traveler, I think that David will easily adapt to a new environment.*
> (means that I am the world traveler)

> *As a newcomer to their city, David's friends fear that he won't understand their customs.*
> (means that David's friends are the newcomer)

While a reader will probably understand the second example (logic tells us that David's friends are not the newcomer to their own city), it doesn't feel right—something seems wrong as soon as we read **David's friends**.

The first example is troublesome because it makes a connection that could be true—that I am a world traveler. How can a reader know what the writer is thinking?

The point is this: whenever you write a phrase beginning with **as**, you have an adjective on the page. Be careful to place it next to the person or thing you want it to describe.

Phrases containing verbals

First of all, what is a verbal? It's a word that comes from a verb but isn't doing the job of a verb. You met one of them earlier in this book (the gerund, an action word ending in *ing* that does the job of a noun). Now it's time to meet the rest of the verbal family:

- **Present participles**—action words ending in *ing*.
  Examples: *planning, anticipating, getting, arriving*

- **Past participles**—action words ending in *ed* (if they're regular) or in various other ways (if they're irregular).
  Examples: *bored, excited, known, understood*

- **Infinitives**—action words preceded by *to*.
  Examples: *to prepare, to adapt, to welcome, to accommodate*

On their own (when they're not preceded by *am, is, was, were*, etc.) participles serve as adjectives. And when placed next to somebody or something, infinitives also serve as adjectives. Take a look at the following sentences.

> *The planning document is in the drawer.*
> (*planning* describes *document*)

> *Planning a trip to Timbuktu, David is understandably nervous.*
> (*Planning* describes *David*)

His <u>bored</u> demeanor camouflages his true feelings.
(***bored*** describes ***demeanor***)

<u>Bored</u> with life in San Francisco, David looks forward to Timbuktu.
(***Bored*** describes ***David***)

<u>To prepare</u> for his trip, David bought many new suitcases.
(***To prepare*** describes ***David***)

<u>To prepare</u> for his arrival in Timbuktu, David's friends cooked up a feast.
(***To prepare*** describes ***David's friends***)

In the first and third examples, the verbals ***planning*** and ***bored*** are serving as simple adjectives to describe ***document*** and ***demeanor***. This should be easy for you to see. But in all the rest of the examples, the verbals are not so easy to see as adjectives because they are part of introductory phrases. The purpose of those phrases is to describe someone or something. That makes each phrase an adjective. And adjectives must be placed next to whatever they are describing.

This is where the common error comes in: people write sentences that open with verbal phrases, but they don't follow them with appropriate subjects. Look what can happen when you don't know you're dealing with an adjective:

> *Anticipating a new adventure, all the suitcases were fully packed.*
>
> *Excited about beginning a new life, David's friends tried their best to be helpful.*
>
> *To accommodate his initial needs, some sacrifices were required.*

All of those sentences open with adjective phrases, yet none of them contains an appropriate subject:

- The first sentence says that all the suitcases are anticipating a new adventure. Now, this could be true in a children's story that attributes human characteristics to things. But we're talking about a dear brother who's moving to Timbuktu, remember?

- The second sentence says that David's friends are excited about beginning a new life. This could also be true, since their lives will change once David arrives in their city. But that's probably not what the writer meant to convey.

- The third sentence says that some sacrifices tried to accommodate David's initial needs, which is quite a stretch. Either David tried to accommodate his own needs by making sacrifices, or his friends tried to accommodate his needs by making sacrifices. Who knows? The meaning of the sentence is up for grabs.

♀ You can avoid all this trouble by

- remembering what participles and infinitives look like

- remembering that they are doing the job of adjectives

- placing them next to whatever you want them to describe.

Adjective Clauses

A clause (a group of words containing a subject and verb) can also serve as an adjective. Anytime you mention somebody or something, no matter where it occurs in your sentence, you can always add some description to it by creating an adjective clause. Adjective clauses begin with the words **who, whom, whose, which, that, where,** and **when.**

Examples:

> *David, who recently moved to Timbuktu, is now looking for a job there.*
> (**who** clause describes **David**)

> *He has recommendations from his friends, whom he is staying with until he gets a job.*
> (**whom** clause describes **friends**)

His friends, <u>whose apartments are small</u>, are praying that David finds employment soon.
(***whose*** clause describes ***friends***)

David is seeking a position <u>whose responsibilities are few.</u>
(***whose*** clause describes ***a position***)

The job he interviewed for yesterday, <u>which doesn't pay very much</u>, is located outside Timbuktu.
(***which*** clause describes ***the job he interviewed for yesterday***)

David prefers a job <u>that he can walk to.</u>
(***that*** clause describes ***a job***)

He'd like to work in a restaurant, <u>where he can have a free meal now and then.</u>
(***where*** clause describes ***a restaurant***)

Ideally, his shift will end at 7:00 p.m., <u>when he is ready for dinner.</u>
(***when*** clause describes ***7:00 p.m.***)

At first reading, you shouldn't notice anything unusual about those examples. Upon closer inspection, you may have a few questions:

• **How can** *whose* **describe** *a position*? **Doesn't** *whose* **always refer to people?**
Whose refers to people and things. It's the only possessive word in the bunch.

- **Why are some adjective clauses set off by commas and others are not?**

  It all depends on the word being described—i.e., the noun or pronoun to the left of the adjective clause. How specific is that word? If it is already specific (for example, **David** or **his friends**), then there's a comma after it, to indicate that the upcoming adjective clause gives extra information. If the noun is not specific (for example, **a position** or **a job**), there's no comma after it because the upcoming adjective clause is now necessary, to make that noun specific. This guideline for using commas applies to all adjective clauses, except those beginning with **which** or **that**.

- **What's the story with** *which* **and** *that*?

  Which and **that** are designated drivers, so to speak. **Which** must drive a clause that gives extra information (because the noun before it is already specific). **That** must drive a clause that gives essential information (because the noun before it is general). So **which** clauses are set off by commas, while **that** clauses are not.

  Examples:

  > *David's job search, which continued for eight months, wore him out.*

  > *A job search that lasts for eight months can wear anybody out.*

There's one more point to make about a ***that*** clause: don't use it to describe people. Use a ***who*** or ***whom*** clause instead.

Typical error:

> *The man that finally hired David is pleased to have a trustworthy new employee.*

> *David is the kind of worker that employers can depend on.*

Corrections:

> *The man who finally hired David is pleased to have a trustworthy new employee.*

> *David is the kind of worker whom employers can depend on.*

Modifier Forms

There are several modifiers that people tend to form incorrectly—they make them plural when they should be singular; they use adverb form when they need adjective form; they type them as one word when they should be two; and they confuse them with words that have similar spellings but different meanings. Following are some prevalent examples.

in regards to   The **s** is wrong. The expression is **in regard to**. (If you want be more concise, you can use **regarding**.)

more importantly   Drop the **ly**. What you're trying to say is that your upcoming point is **more important** than your preceding point.

I feel badly   **Badly** is incorrect. What you feel is **bad**. You wouldn't say, "I feel goodly," would you?

good vs. **well**   **Good** is always an adjective (as in *good car*). **Well** is usually an adverb, describing an action (as in *the car runs well*). The only time that either word fits in the same slot is after a verb coming from **to be** or **to feel**: *I am good, I am well*; *I feel good, I feel well*. (The difference is in meaning—**well** refers to health.) In all other situations, use **good** to describe people, places, and things; use **well** to describe actions.

a vs. **an**   Use **a** or **an**, depending on the sound of the upcoming word. If the word sounds as if it begins with a consonant (*young, university*), use **a** before it. If it sounds as if it begins with a vowel (*egg, MBA*), use **an**.

less vs. *fewer*	**Less** is correct before a mass noun (*less money, less love*). **Fewer** is correct before a countable noun (*fewer items, fewer expenses*).
due to vs. *because of*	**Due to** means "caused by" (*the accident was due to reckless driving*). If **caused by** doesn't fit, use **because of** (*I was late because of heavy traffic*).
complimentary vs. *complementary*	**Complimentary** means "free/no charge," as in *complimentary tickets*. It also means "flattering" or "favorable," as in *complimentary reviews*. **Complementary** refers to the second half of a whole—a remaining part that completes what's missing, as in *complementary angles*.
everyday vs. *every day*	**Everyday** is an adjective that should appear to the left of a noun—as in *everyday activity*. People tend to misuse this one-word form in situations calling for two words. **Every day** is an adverb telling when an action takes place—as in *I swim every day*.
alot vs. *a lot*	This expression is always two words. The one-word version doesn't exist, except as an error.

sometime	***Sometime*** translates into "a day in the
sometimes	future" (*I'll see you sometime*). ***Some-***
some time	***times*** means "every now and then" (*I*
	swim sometimes). ***Some time*** means "a
	block of time" (*I need some time with*
	you).

Only

This versatile modifier deserves to be discussed separately because it is unusual and because people don't understand how important its placement is.

The unusual thing about ***only*** is that it can—and will—modify any noun, verb, phrase, or clause that comes after it. It changes in a flash from an adjective to an adverb and back again, altering the meaning of a sentence every time it moves. Take a look at these examples:

> *Only David is visiting Timbuktu in July because the days are warm then.*
> (no one else is visiting Timbuktu)

> *David is only visiting Timbuktu in July because the days are warm then.*
> (he's just visiting—not staying forever)

> *David is visiting only Timbuktu in July because the days are warm then.*
> (Timbuktu is the sole place he's visiting in July)

David is visiting Timbuktu <u>only in July</u> because the days are warm then.
(he's visiting in no month except July)

David is visiting Timbuktu in July <u>only because</u> the days are warm then.
(he has one reason for visiting)

David is visiting Timbuktu in July because <u>only the days</u> are warm then.
(the days are warm—not the nights)

David is visiting Timbuktu in July because the days are <u>only warm</u> then.
(the days are merely warm—not hot)

David is visiting Timbuktu in July because the days are warm <u>only then.</u>
(there's no other month when the days are warm)

Isn't it amazing how the meaning changes every time ***only*** hops to the right? (Now, that's the kind of modifier I'd like to marry—it has no problem relocating, it finds a new job immediately, and it loves the one it's with.)

The problem with ***only*** is that people tend to throw it into their sentences too soon, rather than waiting for the precise word(s) they want to highlight. They need to understand that ***only*** influences whatever comes next. It sheds light to the right, singling out what follows, altering its meaning. When ***only*** is misplaced, the focus is fuzzy; when **only** is in the right spot, the focus is sharp.

What if someone writes, for example,

> *You should only get married if the right modifier comes along.*

Do you understand what that means? Of course you do. Is the sentence correct? No. It should read,

> *You should get married only if the right modifier comes along.*

What that sentence is trying to say is that there is only one condition under which you should tie the knot: if the right modifier comes along. So **only** needs to appear directly before the **if** clause, not one word sooner. Placing it earlier doesn't cause misunderstanding, but putting it in the right spot creates exactly the right emphasis.

Are there any other modifiers like **only**? Yes. Words like **primarily**, **merely**, **specifically**, **just**, and **mainly** are similar in that they belong directly to the left of what you want them to affect.

For example, don't write

> *I am <u>primarily</u> interested in meeting a rich, eligible modifier*

if what you mean is

> *I am interested <u>primarily</u> in meeting a rich, eligible modifier.*

If you want a bright future with modifiers, you have to treat them right: get to know what they look like, what jobs they can do, where to place them, and how to punctuate them. In return, they'll enhance every sentence you ever write.

QUIZ ON MODIFIERS

Below is a letter to David from his new employer in Tim-buktu. Your job is to edit the letter for modifiers. How are they formed, placed, and punctuated? If the modifiers are correct, leave them alone; if they're not, fix them.

Dear David:

1   After searching for quite sometime, it is my pleasure to have you as the new server at my restaurant. I was getting tired of handling all the tables myself. A man like me who is no spring rooster shouldn't be running around after all the hens, if you know what I mean.

2   I want to warn you that our long-term customers are often short-tempered. If you bring them a dish which they did not order, they may scream at you. Don't feel badly if this happens; bear in mind that you are new and can only handle a few things at a time. In regards to tips, don't worry—I'll give you some cash if I ever run into any.

3	While your job primarily involves serving, you may be asked to cook some times. You mentioned that you know how to prepare certain foods, like rice, beans, and corn. While preparing these delicacies, what ingredients are involved? Do I need to procure any exotic-American spices? I already have an abundant supply of salt and pepper, which may come in handy.

4	As a one man team, your job may sometimes feel overwhelming. If this happens, we can consider shortening your shifts to half hour increments. For example, breakfast can be from 8:00 to 8:30, lunch from 12:00 to 12:30, and dinner from 3:00 to 3:30. That schedule will most likely discourage many of our customers from eating here and you will have more time to relax.

5	I want you to feel welcome in Timbuktu where the people are friendly, the weather is warm, and the salt and pepper are plentiful. More importantly, I hope you decide to make this your permanent home. We need people, who are willing to work in various capacities and in half hour shifts.

6	I look forward to seeing you everyday.

	Your new employer

ANSWERS TO MODIFIERS QUIZ

- Paragraph 1 contains three errors. In the first sentence, *sometime* should be two words; the subject of the clause should be *I*, not *it* (the opening verbal phrase, *After searching . . .* , is an adjective that must be followed by the person it describes). In the third sentence, there should be commas around the *who* clause because that clause provides extra information.

- Paragraph 2 contains five errors. In the first sentence, *short-tempered* should not be hyphenated because it follows the noun it describes. In the second sentence, *which* should be *that* because it introduces an essential clause (the noun before it, *a dish*, is general). In the third sentence, *badly* should be *bad*; *only* should appear before *a few things*, not before *handles*. In the fourth sentence, *regards* should be *regard*.

- Paragraph 3 contains four errors. In the first sentence, *primarily* should appear before *serving*, not before *involves*; *some times* should be *sometimes*. In the third sentence, the subject following the opening descriptive phrase should be *you*, not *ingredients* (*While preparing . . .* describes a person, not ingredients). In the fifth sentence, there should be no hyphen in *exotic-American*.

- Paragraph 4 contains three errors. In the first sentence, *one man* should be hyphenated; the subject of the clause should be *you*, not *your job* (the *As* phrase describes a person, not a job). In the second sentence, *half hour* should be hyphenated.

- Paragraph 5 contains four errors. In the first sentence, there should be a comma after *Timbuktu* (the *where* clause is extra, not essential, after the specific noun *Timbuktu*). In the second sentence, *more importantly* should be *more important*. In the third sentence, there should be no comma after *people* (the *who* clause is necessary after the generic word *people*); *half hour* should be hyphenated.

- Paragraph 6 contains one error. The last word should be two words: *every day*, not *everyday*.

Chapter 6: Connectives

So far, you've learned a few things about people, places, and things (nouns and pronouns); about actions (verbs); and about descriptions (modifiers). What's left? Glue and road signs. To hold ideas together, we use words that can join (glue). To show where a discussion is headed next, we use words that indicate a change in direction (road signs). All of these words are referred to, in general, as *connectives*. Specifically, they are prepositions, conjunctions, and adverbs.

Prepositions

Prepositions are usually small words that indicate position (*in, on, under, over*) or relationship (*of, for, to, from*).

If your native tongue is not English, prepositions are a major challenge since their use is as various as the words they accompany. It's not easy, for example, to remember that the noun **discussion** is followed by the preposition **about** (*we had a discussion about bananas*), yet the verb **discuss** requires no preposition (*we discussed bananas*); similarly, the noun **request** is followed by the preposition *for* (*we submitted a request for bananas*), yet the verb **request** requires no preposition (*we requested bananas*). It's also not easy to understand why we get on a bus, on a train, on a plane, yet in a car. Or why we are on a team and on a committee but in a group. Often there's no logic behind our use of prepositions; there's only the use itself to take note of.

If your native tongue is English, you manage most prepositions correctly without thinking about it. Your ear is your guide, and typically it's a good one. There are a few things, however, that your ear may need to hear about.

Like I said

People handle **like** correctly when it's a verb (as in *I like bananas* or *I would like a banana*). They don't always use it correctly as a connective.

Common error:

> *Like I said, bananas are popular around the world.*

Correct:

> *As I said, bananas are popular around the world.*

You need to use *as* when a subject and verb are coming up. *Like* is a preposition; prepositions introduce phrases. *As*, in this case, is a conjunction; conjunctions introduce clauses. Here are some more sentences, to help you understand the difference between *like* and *as*.

Examples:

> *Eating fruits like pomegranates requires time and patience.*
>
> *Like many a primate, I prefer bananas.*
>
> *As any monkey knows, bananas are quite agreeable.*
>
> *Pomegranates, as I told you, are demanding.*

Considered as

Whenever you're saying that someone or something is **considered** a certain way, don't use *as*.

Common error:

> *She is considered as honest.*
>
> *The Taj Mahal is considered as an architectural wonder.*

Correct:

> *She is considered honest.*
>
> *The Taj Mahal is considered an architectural wonder.*

Different than

The connective to use after **different** is **from**, not **than**. **Than** is correct after a comparative word—for example, *taller than, younger than, more complicated than, less expensive than*. **Different** is not a comparative word. When you're classifying something as different, you're not saying it is more than or less than; you're saying simply that it is not the same. So one thing is always different from another.

Fascinated but afraid of

Sometimes two words in a sentence need to be followed by two different prepositions. When that happens, be sure to include them both.

Common error:

The child was fascinated but afraid of lizards.

Correct:

The child was fascinated by but afraid of lizards.

Something else about which to talk

Contrary to what a well-meaning teacher may have told you in elementary school, there is nothing wrong with ending a sentence in a preposition. Furthermore, there never has been anything wrong with doing so. If a sentence ends in a word that requires a preposition after it, use that preposition. Don't look for some other way to say it; what you wind up with may sound stuffy.

Stuffy:

> *We need to find something else about which to talk.*

Natural:

> *We need to find something else to talk about.*

Look forward to see, committed to keep, prone to forget, on my way to buy

Many people misunderstand the grammar of these four expressions: they treat **to** as if it were the beginning of an infinitive (*to see, to keep, to forget, to buy*). It isn't. It's a preposition that must be followed by an object—i.e., a noun or a gerund. No one makes a mistake when they need a noun (*I look forward to lunch* or *I am committed to monogamy*); they err when they need a gerund—an action word ending in **ing**.

Common error:

> *I look forward to see you.*

> *I am committed to keep my promise.*

I am prone to forget what I say.

I am on my way to buy roses for you.

Correct:

I look forward to seeing you.

I am committed to keeping my promise.

I am prone to forgetting what I say.

I am on my way to buying roses for you.

Conjunctions

Conjunctions are words with glue on them, meaning that they have the capacity to join. There are three types of conjunctions—coordinating, subordinating, and correlative. Even though they all do the job of gluing sentence parts together, their roles and their effects vary. So do the problems that people have with them.

Coordinating conjunctions

These are the most common and versatile glue words in our language, the ones you first learned to use: **and**, **but**, **yet**, **so**, **nor**, **or**, and **for**. (**For**, in this instance, means "because," as in *I was late to work, for there was a lot of traffic.*)

Coordinating conjunctions can join anything—words, phrases, or clauses. Whatever they join, the result is a list— items in a series. When you write items in a series, you need to make sure they match each other in terms of form. This is the rule of parallel structure.

Common error:

> I like bananas because they are delicious, nutritious, and they help me fall asleep.
>
> You can buy bananas at the supermarket, the farmers' market, or from roadside vendors.
>
> Bananas taste good, they are good for you, but won't help you stay awake.

Correct:

> I like bananas because they are delicious, nutritious, and conducive to sleep.
>
> You can buy bananas at the supermarket, at the farmers' market, or from roadside vendors.
>
> Bananas taste good, they are good for you, but they won't help you stay awake.

It doesn't matter how many items are involved or what part of speech they are; it also doesn't matter whether the items are marching across the page or down the page. What matters is that they are parallel—all the same kind of word, the same kind of phrase, the same kind of clause. Once you understand this rule, your ear can help you write items in a series that sound alike.

Another issue that crops up here is punctuation. How do you punctuate items joined by coordinating conjunctions? The answer depends on the number and the type of items.

If the number is two and the items are not independent clauses, you do not punctuate.

Examples:

> *After eating several bananas, I feel <u>happy</u> and <u>drowsy</u>.*
>
> *Bananas are good <u>at home</u> or <u>at the office</u>.*
>
> *If you're working, you may want to avoid a fruit that <u>tastes good</u> but <u>puts you to sleep</u>.*

If the number is three or more, you place a comma after each item in the series, even the item before the conjunction.

Examples:

> *After eating several bananas, I feel <u>happy</u>, <u>drowsy</u>, and <u>full</u>.*
>
> *Bananas are good <u>at home</u>, <u>at the office</u>, or <u>at the beach</u>.*
>
> *If you're working, you may want to avoid a fruit that <u>tastes good</u>, <u>fills you up</u>, but <u>puts you to sleep</u>.*

If a coordinating conjunction joins two independent clauses, you have four punctuation options.

Examples:

> *I eat a lot of bananas and I've recommended them to my friends.*

> *My friends like bananas, but they can live without them.*

> *Bananas won't disagree with your stomach; nor will they talk back.*

> *I never met a banana I didn't like. Yet some are rather spoiled, I must admit.*

The last two punctuation options are possible because a coordinating conjunction doesn't affect the independence of a clause. That is, independent clauses that begin with coordinating conjunctions are still independent, which means that they can take a semicolon or period to the left of them.

Why would you want to punctuate like that? For effect. You may want to convey that the upcoming clause is the second half of a two-part story. Or you may want to give it maximum attention by making it a new sentence.

Why, then, would you need the conjunction? For meaning. Conjunctions carry meaning as well as glue. They tell how the upcoming clause is related to the previous clause. (When a reader sees *yet*, for example, he knows that contrast will follow; when he sees *so*, he knows that a result is coming; when he sees *or*, he gets ready for an alternative; and so forth.)

The way you punctuate depends on how you want your second clause to be perceived:

- If you want the second clause to be read without a pause, don't punctuate.

- If you want a slight pause after your opening clause, use a comma.

- If you want your two clauses to appear as two halves of a whole, place a semicolon between them.

- If you want your second clause to receive maximum attention, type a period, to make a new sentence out of it.

Subordinating conjunctions

There are many more subordinating conjunctions in English than there are coordinating. Here are the most common: *although, even though, whereas, while, because, since, as, in that, in order that, as long as, if, unless, provided that, once, until, when, whenever, before, after, as if, as though.*

Because they are conjunctions, subordinators carry glue. What they most often glue together are clauses. When they do this job, the result is one major clause and one minor clause—that is, one independent clause and one dependent clause. The dependent clause is the one beginning with the subordinating conjunction.

Examples:

> *I'm still writing about bananas, even though they're starting to bore me.*

> *My mind is stuck on bananas as if there were no other topic.*

> *If I change topics now, you may miss the bananas.*

You'll notice that, besides making one clause dependent on the other, subordinating conjunctions differ from coordinating in terms of positioning: they can join two clauses by showing up in the middle of them or by appearing at the beginning of a sentence.

You'll also notice that, when a subordinate clause is involved, your punctuation options are limited. If you look back at the last three examples, you'll see either a comma or no punctuation. (You won't see a semicolon or period because there aren't two independent clauses.)

• The comma is optional when the subordinate clause <u>follows</u> the independent clause (first and second examples).

• The comma is customary when the subordinate clause <u>introduces</u> the independent clause (third example).

Correlative conjunctions

Despite their fancy name, these word pairs are quite familiar to you. They are the two-part conjunctions you use when you want special emphasis as well as glue:

either . . . or

neither . . . nor

not only . . . but also

not . . . but

The only problem that people have when using these connectives is that they don't place them in the right spot for parallel structure. Each double conjunction can join any two elements within a sentence (words, phrases, or clauses); but the elements being joined must match each other. (This is the same rule that pertains to items in a series joined by coordinating conjunctions.)

Common error:

Chiquita either <u>eats</u> bananas at home or <u>on the road</u>.

Neither <u>are they</u> her <u>favorite food</u> nor <u>part</u> of the low-carb diet she should be following.

She not only <u>eats</u> them because they are convenient but also <u>free</u>.

Chiquita is not <u>interested</u> in the weight she should lose but <u>in the money</u> she can save.

Correct:

> *Chiquita eats bananas either <u>at home</u> or <u>on the road</u>.*

> *They are neither her favorite <u>food</u> nor <u>part</u> of the low-carb diet she should be following.*

> *She eats them because they are not only <u>convenient</u> but also <u>free</u>.*

> *Chiquita is interested not <u>in the weight</u> she should lose but <u>in the money</u> she can save.*

In all of those examples (erroneous and correct), the words following each conjunction are underlined. If you compare the underlined items in the first set of sentences, you'll see that they don't match:

> **eats** and **on the road**

> **are they her favorite food** and **part**

> **eats** and **free**

> **interested** and **in the money.**

If you compare the underlined items in the second set of sentences, you'll see that they do match:

> **at home** and **on the road**

> **food** and **part**

> **convenient** and **free**

> **in the weight** and **in the money.**

The issue here is placement, rather than form. When using double conjunctions, people usually form their items correctly but don't know where to put the connectives. The connectives must appear directly to the left of the items they're meant to join. You can't toss them in before your sentence is ready for them.

When Shakespeare wrote, "Ripeness is all," he must have been thinking about correlative conjunctions. Or maybe he was thinking about bananas.

Conjunctive Adverbs

Conjunctive adverbs are very common—you see them all the time and you use them frequently. Here's what they look like:

however, nevertheless, rather, instead, otherwise, on the other hand, alternatively

furthermore, moreover, besides, additionally, similarly

therefore, thus, consequently, hence

previously, now, initially, presently, then, next, still, meanwhile, subsequently, finally, afterward

indeed, in fact, of course, accordingly, anyhow, anyway, frankly, certainly

Several of these words end in *ly*, reminding you that they belong to the adverb family. But how can you remember that all of these words are adverbs? And why should you?

Actually, it's not important what you call these words as long as you know they are not conjunctions—i.e., they have no glue on them and therefore can't join anything with anything. They are transition words that show how ideas are related. They serve as road signs. They offer helpful information and add fluency to your discussion. But they don't join.

So if your sentence contains two independent clauses and the second one begins with an adverb, you still need a joining technique. A comma cannot do that job. What you need is a semicolon.

Common error:

> *Chiquita wears a hat filled with bananas, however, she manages to keep her balance.*

Correct:

> *Chiquita wears a hat filled with bananas; however, she manages to keep her balance.*

(You may also place a period between those clauses, but then you won't be joining them.)

Besides carrying no glue, adverbs differ from conjunctions in two other ways:

• Adverbs can introduce a clause, interrupt a clause, or end a clause. (Conjunctions can only introduce a clause.)

Examples:

> *Chiquita is usually well mannered; <u>however</u>, sometimes she eats out of her hat.*

> *Chiquita is usually well mannered; sometimes, <u>however</u>, she eats out of her hat.*

> *Chiquita is usually well mannered; sometimes she eats out of her hat, <u>however</u>.*

• Adverbs are followed by commas. (No conjunction is followed by a comma, even when it begins a sentence.)

Connectives Leading to Examples or Explanations

To tell your reader that you're about to give an example or a full explanation, you offer road signs: **like, such as, including, for instance, for example (e.g.), that is (i.e.), namely, specifically.**

The problems people have with these connectives relate to punctuation and usage.

Punctuation

The first three expressions—*like*, *such as*, and *including*—may be preceded by commas (if the upcoming example isn't essential), but they are never followed by commas.

Common error:

> *I enjoy snacks like, bananas.*
>
> *I enjoy snacks such as, bananas.*
>
> *I enjoy a variety of snacks including, bananas.*

Correct:

> *I enjoy snacks like bananas.*
>
> *I enjoy snacks such as bananas.*
>
> *I enjoy a variety of snacks, including bananas.*

The last five expressions—*for instance*, *for example*, *that is*, *namely*, and *specifically*—are always followed by commas, no matter what punctuation sets them apart from the rest of the sentence.

Examples:

> *There are some strange things in Chiquita's hat—for instance, bananas.*
>
> *From her hat Chiquita retrieves a snack (for example, bananas).*

There is something fruity about Chiquita's hat—that is, bananas.

The contents of Chiquita's hat (namely, bananas) are curious.

They're wondering what they are doing in such a strange place—specifically, a hat.

Usage

People often use the abbreviation *i.e.* without knowing what it means. *I.e.* stands for *id est*, Latin words meaning "that is." *That is* must lead to a <u>full explanation</u>. The error occurs when people use *i.e.* to mean "for example."

The abbreviation that means "for example" is *e.g.* It stands for the Latin words *exempli gratia.*

Finally, both of these abbreviations need to be punctuated correctly. Each letter is followed by a period, and the second period is followed by a comma. The periods indicate that the expression is an abbreviation; the comma indicates that the expression is introductory.

Examples:

Chiquita's hat serves a practical purpose—i.e., it contains her lunch.

Chiquita's hat serves many purposes—e.g., it keeps her head straight while everyone else is thinking about bananas.

Confusing Pairs

If vs. *whether*

If introduces a condition; **whether** introduces a choice. The common error is that people use **if** when they mean **whether**—for example, *We need to determine if Chiquita's hat is affecting banana sales* versus *We need to determine whether Chiquita's hat is affecting banana sales.*

One way to test your use of **if** is to say "or not" after it. If your sentence makes sense when you insert **or not**, the connective you need is **whether**. (You needn't keep **or not** in your sentence—it's implied by **whether**.)

Here are some verbs that typically lead to **whether**: *determine, decide, know, wonder, find out, investigate, discern, learn, discover, understand, question, see, ask, check.*

Then vs. *than*

Then refers to time, as in *now and then*; **than** is for comparisons, as in *more than* or *less than*.

Redundancies

Etc. after *such as*

If you introduce some examples with **such as**, don't use **etc.** at the end of the list. **Such as** means that your list contains examples, not the full story. **Etc.** means the same.

Nor in the same clause as *no* or *not*

If you use **no** or **not**, don't use **nor** within the same clause. Use **or**, instead.

Incorrect:

> *I don't want a pomegranate nor a banana.*

Correct:

> *I don't want a pomegranate or a banana.*

The reason why is because

Don't follow **reason** with **why** or **because**—that's saying the same thing three times. Drop **why**; use **that** instead of **because**.

Incorrect:

> *The reason why I am late is because I paused to eat a*
> *pomegranate.*

Correct:

> *The reason I am late is that I paused to eat a*
> *pomegranate.*

As you've seen, using connectives correctly is often tricky business. It calls for awareness of many rules related to usage, form, grammar, and punctuation. Is it worth it? Why not avoid all those troublesome glue words and write only simple, elementary sentences?

The answer is that your sentences will wind up being, well ... simple and elementary. They'll deliver main points but they won't show relationships, indicate chronology, or signal changes in direction. Your reader will have to guess at the connections that you failed to provide.

Take a look at a group of related sentences written without connectives:

> *Chiquita wears a hat. The hat is filled. The filling is*
> *fruit. The hat is heavy. It is difficult to balance. She can't*
> *remove the hat. She needs relief. She must unload the*

> *fruit. Wearing the hat is not her preference. She must*
> *continue to wear it. She wants to keep her job.*

Those sentences should, of course, be combined—to avoid repetition of key words and to show how the ideas relate to one another. For example,

> *Chiquita's hat is heavy and difficult to balance because*
> *it is filled with fruit. She can't remove it, to gain some*
> *relief, without first unloading the fruit. Although wear-*
> *ing the hat is not her preference, she must continue to do*
> *so if she wants to keep her job.*

Now, that paragraph won't win any literary prize, but it's a lot easier to read than the original string of isolated sentences. The increased fluency comes largely from adding five garden-variety connectives: ***and***, ***because***, ***without***, ***although***, and ***if***.

Connectives go a long way in enhancing the meaning and flow of your text. They're well worth including, with all their special effects and idiosyncrasies.

QUIZ ON CONNECTIVES

Below is a letter from Chiquita to her employer, the banana boss. Your job is to edit the letter for connectives—words that serve as glue or as road signs. Are they the right words? Are the sentences punctuated correctly? If so, leave the text as it is; if not, fix it.

Dear Top Banana:

1   Because I have been representing the company for so many years people think of me as a bunch of bananas. I had thought it wasn't bothering me until I began to see bananas whenever I looked into a mirror.

2   Recently I saw a psychologist to find out who I really am—i.e., a person or a logo. Surely you can understand my confusion: my name is on every banana you sell, in every commercial you make and every truck that transports your product. Furthermore,

when people see me they don't look at my face nor my outfit; they stare only at my hat. The reason why, of course, is the bananas. I am considered as nothing more than a one-dimensional fruit. While this is an understandable consequence of pervasive market-ing; I'm having trouble with it. But, like I said, I'm working on the problem with my therapist as I'm committed to solve it.

3   I'm writing to suggest that either you add someone else's name to your product or add some other fruits to my hat. You could call the product "Chiquita and Jean-Paul"; for example, which may bring you increased business in France. Or, you could throw a few kumquats into my hat, to show that I'm more then just bananas.

4   Any change will take time to implement, however, the result will be worth it. Your customers will have something new to focus and talk about. And I may be able to see my own face in the mirror again.

5   The problem I'm having is different than any I've ever known. It bothers me not only during the day but also keeps me awake at night. (Please don't advise me to eat a banana before bedtime.)

Chiquita

ANSWERS TO CONNECTIVES QUIZ

- Paragraph 1 contains one error. In the first sentence, there should be a comma after *years* because that marks the end of an introductory subordinate clause. (In the second sentence, the lack of punctuation after the opening clause is fine: a comma isn't mandatory when the first clause is independent and the second is subordinate.)

- Paragraph 2 contains ten errors. In the second sentence, there should be a comma after the introductory adverb *surely*; there should be a comma after *make* (the second item in a series of three); the preposition *on* should precede *every truck* (to make this third item parallel with the preceding two items). In the third sentence, there should be a comma after *me*; *nor* should be *or* (because it's in the same clause as *don't*). In the fourth sentence, *why* should be deleted (because it's redundant after *reason*). In the fifth sentence, *as* should be deleted. In the sixth sentence, the semicolon should be a comma (because the opening clause is subordinate).

In the seventh sentence, *like* should be *as*; *solve* should be *solving*.

• Paragraph 3 contains five errors. In the first sentence, *either* should be moved two words to the right, so that it precedes *someone else's name* (the first of two choices); the second mention of *add* should be deleted so that *or* precedes *some other fruits* (the second choice). The result of this revision is good parallel structure: *... that you add either someone else's name to your product or some other fruits to my hat.* In the second sentence, the semicolon should be a comma, to mark the beginning of an interruption. In the third sentence, there should be no punctuation after *Or*; *then* should be *than*.

• Paragraph 4 contains two errors. In the first sentence, there should be a semicolon before *however*, not a comma. In the second sentence, *focus* should be followed by *on*.

• Paragraph 5 contains two errors. In the first sentence, *different* should be followed by *from*, not *than*. In the second sentence, *not only* should be moved to the left of *bothers* (for parallel structure: *not only bothers ... but also keeps ...*).

Chapter 7: Punctuation

Punctuation marks are to writing what vocal delivery is to speech. Can you imagine talking in a monotone without pause? Your audience would have difficulty making sense of your words, let alone figuring out where emphasis and nuance belong.

If you drain the punctuation from your writing, you have no louds, no softs, no expression, no innuendo. If you use only a few punctuation marks, you seriously restrict your style. If you misuse punctuation marks, you send your reader down the wrong road, maybe even up a tree.

You need to understand exactly what each mark can and cannot do, as well as the message it gives to your reader. There aren't that many marks—fifteen in all. And some are so familiar (periods, question marks) or so seldom necessary (slashes, brackets, ellipses) that the number you need to know by heart is only nine.

Nine is not a lot. But the benefits of understanding these nine are countless.

Commas

Besides incidental jobs (like separating the day from the year in a date), commas play four roles within a sentence:

1. **they separate items in a series of three or more**

2. **they surround an interruption**

3. **they show where an introduction ends**

4. **they mark the beginning of an afterthought or final qualifier.**

Separating items in a series of three or more

Examples:

> *New lockers, bins, racks, and shelves will be added to the ark.*

> *We will hammer, nail, coax, and cajole until the construction is complete.*

> *The result will be a vessel that is logically designed, well organized, and visually attractive.*

COMMON QUESTIONS:

- **Is the comma necessary after the next-to-last item —the item before** *and*?

While some professional publications (*The New Yorker*) include it and others (*Time Magazine*) tend to leave it out, the rule is still to place a comma after every item in a series of three or more. This practice makes sense: with a comma after every item, each gets equal treatment; no item looks more closely related to another because of missing punctuation. Also, leaving out that last comma can cause confusion. For example,

> *The ark-building manual gives information on analyzing and solving construction problems, avoiding the hazards of welding and staying afloat into old age.*

How many topics does that book discuss—two or three? A comma after ***welding*** makes it clear:

> *The ark-building manual gives information on analyzing and solving construction problems, avoiding the hazards of welding, and staying afloat into old age.*

- **Are commas necessary after items in a vertical series?**

Not really. When items are marching across the page, commas show where one stops and the next begins. When items are marching down the page, bullets (or numbers or letters) accomplish that job. Why do it twice?

Example:

The renovated ark will boast many new features:

- *lockers for valuables*

- *bins for trash*

- *racks for equipment*

- *shelves for books.*

Note: There's a period at the end of the final item, to mark the end of the sentence.

- **What if each item in a vertical series is a complete thought? Is punctuation or capitalization necessary?**

How you punctuate and whether you capitalize depend on the emphasis you want.

If you want each item to be seen as a continuation of the overall sentence, don't punctuate until the end of the last item and don't capitalize at all.

Example:

We are renovating the ark for several reasons:

- *valuables must be protected*

- *trash must be contained*

- *equipment must be organized and easy to find*

- *books must be elevated.*

If you want the items to receive maximum attention as separate points, then treat each as a new sentence, capitalizing at the beginning and placing a period at the end.

Example:

We are renovating the ark for several reasons:

- *Valuables must be protected.*

- *Trash must be contained.*

- *Equipment must be organized and easy to find.*

- *Books must be elevated.*

Surrounding an interruption

Examples:

Our new ark, finally, is a beautiful sight to behold.

This vessel, completely remodeled, is ready for passengers.

The number of passengers, which I've yet to determine, must be even.

Note: An interruption can be a word, a phrase, or a clause.

COMMON QUESTION:

- **Are commas the only way to punctuate an interruption?**

No, but they are the most common way. Commas give the interruption normal attention. If you want to give an interruption maximum attention, use a dash to the left and right of it. If you want to give it minimum attention (if you want it to read like an aside comment, as does this interruption), use parentheses around it.

Ending an introduction

Examples:

> *First, I'll compose a passenger list.*

> *Resisting the urge to include every single acquaintance, I'll limit the list to couples.*

> *Although some couples may be odd, the number of passengers will be even.*

Note: An introduction can be a word, a phrase, or a clause.

Beginning an afterthought or final qualifier

Examples:

> *The gathering will be lively, surely.*

> *The guests will chatter and squawk, getting to know one another.*

> *The event may go down in history, as long as someone keeps a log.*

Note: An afterthought or final qualifier can be a word, a phrase, or a clause.

COMMON QUESTION:

- **Is a comma the only way to set off an afterthought or final qualifier?**

No. Here again, you may use a dash or parentheses to distinguish nonessential material from a main idea. A dash gives your final words maximum attention; parentheses give them minimum attention.

Semicolons

Semicolons perform two jobs:

1. **they join two closely related complete thoughts (independent clauses)**

2. **they separate items in a series when the items contain commas or are unusually long.**

Joining two closely related complete thoughts
Examples:

> *Jonah reacts quickly and impulsively to situations; Job looks before he leaps.*

> *Patience is a virtue; it is also an art.*

After being swallowed by a whale, Jonah had a lot of time to think; he began to understand the wisdom of looking before leaping.

Some impulsive acts are harmless; others have confining consequences.

Separating items in a series when the items contain commas or are unusually long

Examples:

This story involves Jonah, who becomes close with a whale; Job, who loses his shirt; Adam, who covers for a fig leaf; and Eve, who falls for a snake.

The plot gets complicated as Jonah gets to know his captor from the inside out; as Job considers Zen Buddhism; as Adam cannot find an alibi for the fig leaf; and as Eve, usually levelheaded, accepts counsel from a cottonmouth.

Colons

A colon tells the reader that you're about to specifically explain a general statement. The general statement, to the left of your colon, must be a complete thought (independent clause). The specific explanation, to the right of your colon, can be in any form—a word, a phrase, a clause, or a series of items.

Examples:

> *As a student, Noah had difficulty in one subject: trigonometry.*
>
> *Trigonometry is easy for some people: those who understand triangles.*
>
> *Triangles perplexed Noah: no matter how he viewed them, he couldn't tell which end was up.*
>
> *Noah tried valiantly to raise his trigonometry grade: he studied more, he brought apples to his teacher, and he prayed a great deal.*

Note: Don't capitalize after a colon unless you're writing an independent clause—and, even in that case, capitalizing is optional.

Dashes

First of all, a dash is not a hyphen. It is twice as long (you need to hit the hyphen key twice to create one dash) and it performs very different functions.

Dashes do three jobs, each of which can be accomplished by another punctuation mark. Why, then, use dashes?

Because they carry two messages—one related to the job they are doing and the other related to emphasis, clarity, or formality. Here are the roles of dashes:

1. **they surround an interruption**

2. **they lead to an afterthought**

3. **they introduce a specific explanation.**

Surrounding an interruption

Examples:

> *My daughter—Rebecca—has an imaginary playmate.*
>
> *My neighbor's children—Sima, Sarah, and Sam—interact with the real kids on our block.*

Note: In the first example, the dashes give the interruption more emphasis than commas or parentheses would. In the second example, the dashes lend more clarity than commas would, since the interruption contains commas.

Leading to an afterthought

Examples:

> *Rebecca speaks to her friend in a private language—one that I don't understand.*
>
> *Her friend replies with abundant good humor—at least, that's the way it appears.*

Note: Although in the first example a comma could lead to the afterthought, the dash gives it more emphasis. In the second example, the dash lends both emphasis and clarity (using commas before and after **at least** would make it look like an interruption, which it isn't).

Introducing a specific explanation

Examples:

> *Rebecca has a name for her playmate—Stefan Stefanopolis.*
>
> *Stefan has one great quality—he makes Rebecca laugh.*

Note: While a colon or parentheses may also be used to distinguish an explanation, the dash creates a different effect: it is less formal than a colon; it gives more attention to the explanation than parentheses.

Hyphens

Hyphens connect multiple adjectives that appear to the left of a noun. What is a multiple adjective? Two or more descriptive words that need each other to create the meaning you want—for example, **blue-eyed boy**: he is not a blue boy or an eyed boy; **blue** and **eyed** must be linked, to make proper sense.

Furthermore, ***blue-eyed*** is hyphenated because it appears to the left of ***boy***. If it appeared to the right, it would not be hyphenated—for example, *the boy is blue eyed.*

More examples:

> *nine-hole golf course*
>
> *300-page book*
>
> *no-nonsense approach*
>
> *life-affirming goals*
>
> *labor-intensive work*
>
> *vine-ripened tomatoes*
>
> *58-year-old senator*
>
> *off-the-record comment*
>
> *four- and six-part harmony*

Note: Don't hyphenate when the first descriptive word is an adverb ending in ***ly***—for example, ***poorly written script*** or ***highly regarded institution.***

Parentheses

Parentheses are for surrounding background information, aside comments, material of secondary importance.

They de-emphasize the text they contain; they prompt the reader to lower her voice until she exits the parenthetical remark.

Parentheses can occur within a sentence, referring to a given word or phrase; at the end of a clause, referring to the entire statement; or around an upcoming new sentence. (In other words, they can surround an interruption, an afterthought, or a sentence, like the one you're reading now.)

Examples:

> *Apparently, Stefan Stefanopolis (my daughter's imaginary playmate) is quite amusing.*
>
> *He keeps Rebecca laughing throughout the day (and sometimes into the night).*
>
> *I'm a little worried that Rebecca doesn't know what's real and what's not. (This morning she asked me why I hadn't served Stefan any pancakes.)*

Note: The second and third examples show that a period can go either outside or inside the closing parenthesis, depending on what just ended—a sentence containing a parenthetical remark or a separate sentence within parentheses.

Double Quotation Marks

Double quotation marks do four jobs:

1. **they surround words spoken or written by someone else**

2. **they surround words used as terms** (this purpose can also be served by italics)

3. **they surround words used sarcastically**

4. **they surround titles of chapters or articles** (in contrast, titles of books and periodicals are underlined or italicized).

Surrounding words spoken or written by someone else

Examples:

> *Patrick Henry said, "Give me liberty or give me death."*

> *When he mentioned "liberty," was he, by any chance, married?*

Note: In the first example, there's a comma after **Patrick Henry said** because those are introductory words leading to a quoted <u>sentence</u>.

In the second example, there is no punctuation after **When he mentioned** because what follows is only one quoted <u>word</u> (not a quoted sentence).

Note: Periods and commas belong <u>inside</u> closing quotation marks, no matter what. Don't even think of placing them outside—just tuck them in.

Surrounding words used as terms

Example:

> *What do you suppose "liberty" meant to Mr. Henry?*
> (meaning "the term liberty")

Surrounding words used sarcastically (to achieve the effect of *so-called*)

Example:

> *People in many countries enjoy the "liberty" of voting for the only candidate on the ballot.*

Note: Sarcasm is the effect you wind up with if you use quotes where they don't belong. Quotes are not for showing your discomfort with a colloquial expression. Either make your peace with the idiom and use it without quotes, or choose another way to say what you mean.

Incorrect:

> *Please don't "beat around the bush."*

Correct:

> *Please don't beat around the bush.*

or

> *Please get to the point.*

Surrounding titles of chapters or articles

Examples:

> *Did you read "Bush on Fire" in Time Magazine?*

> *No, but I read "My Dungeon Shook" in The Fire Next Time.*

COMMON QUESTION:

- **If commas and periods always belong inside closing quotation marks, what about colons, semicolons, question marks, and exclamation points? Do they belong inside or out?**

Colons and semicolons belong outside the closing quotation mark because they belong to the overall sentence, rather than to the words in quotes. (It wouldn't make sense to stop a quote at a colon or semicolon.)

Examples:

I think I know what Patrick Henry meant when he said, "Give me liberty or give me death": he was expressing a desire to be single again.

Mr. Henry didn't really mean "give me death"; he meant that if he couldn't divorce, he'd move to New Jersey.

Question marks and exclamation points belong either inside or outside the closing quotation mark, depending on what they belong to—the words in quotes or the overall sentence. In rare instances, a question mark appears before and after the quote.

Examples:

Consider the song "What's Love Got to Do with It?"

Do you agree that love is "a second-hand emotion"?

What's the message within "What's Love Got to Do with It?"?

It may be "A heart can be broken!"

It can't be "Love is a sweet old-fashioned notion"!

Note: When a sentence that isn't a question ends with a quotation that is a question (*Consider the song "What's Love Got to Do with It?"*), don't use a period. Even though the overall sentence is not a question, it simply ends when that question mark shows up. No more punctuation.

Single Quotation Marks

A single quotation mark (the same symbol used to create an apostrophe) serves only one purpose: to surround a quotation that occurs <u>inside</u> another quotation. Since double quotation marks encompass the overall quote, you need another way to distinguish the quote within.

Example:

> *The instructor said, "Whenever I explain punctuation, someone asks, 'What's the purpose of single quotes?'"*

Note: The example ends with both a single and a double quote because both quotations finish at the same time.

Apostrophes

Apostrophes serve three purposes:

1. **they represent a missing letter within a contraction**

2. **they make a noun possessive**

3. **they make an abbreviation, a letter, or a numeral plural.**

Representing a missing letter within a contraction

Example:

> *It's acceptable to use contractions in business writing if you want to achieve a conversational tone.*

Making a noun possessive

The way to make a noun possessive depends on whether the noun ends in the letter *s*. It doesn't matter whether that noun is singular or plural; what matters is its final letter.

Here's the rule: If the noun does not end in the letter *s*, make it possessive by adding an apostrophe and an *s*. If the noun does end in the letter *s*, add only an apostrophe.

Examples:

> *the mouse's tail*
>
> *the mice's tails*
>
> *the platypus' bill*
>
> *the platypuses' bills*

The first two examples are made possessive in the same way (apostrophe *s*), even though one is singular and the other is plural. The third and fourth examples are also made possessive in the same way (only an apostrophe), even though one is singular and the other is plural.

The only time you have the option of adding an apostrophe and an *s* to a noun that ends in an *s* is when that noun is someone's name—e.g., *Myers's rum.* Remember, that extra *s* is an option; it is also correct to write *Myers' rum.*

Making an abbreviation, a letter, or a numeral plural

Example:

> *The teaching assistants (TA's) predicted several B's on student-grade reports and a few 10's on instructor-performance evaluations.*

Note: The apostrophe may also be omitted in the plural form of abbreviations, letters, and numerals—for example, *TAs, Bs, 10s.*

Ellipses

An ellipsis (. . .) indicates that something has been deleted from a quote. It doesn't tell how much has been left out; it shows only that the passage has been reduced to its pertinent parts.

Example:

> **Original text:** *"San Francisco's American Conservatory Theater (ACT), the nation's only full-time resident repertory company,*

> *has a considerably scaled-down season*
> *this year."*

Abridged text: *"San Francisco's American Conserva-*
tory Theater . . . has a considerably
scaled-down season this year."

Note: If the ellipsis leads to the end of a sentence, follow it
with a space and then a final period.

Brackets

Brackets ([ ]) are the opposite of ellipses—they show that
something has been added to or changed within quoted
material. They come in handy when you want to clarify
something for your reader.

Example:

Original text: *"Millions of genes are arranged along*
the giant strands of DNA in each
human cell."

Enhanced text: *"Millions of genes are arranged along*
the giant strands of DNA [commonly
known as chromosomes] in each
human cell."

Slashes

A slash (/) means "and or."

Example:

She is the manager/maintenance person of this ark.

Question Marks

Besides ending an interrogatory sentence, a question mark can turn a declarative statement into an inquiry.

Examples:

What do you do for relaxation?

You call exercise relaxing?

Exclamation Points

An exclamation point indicates enthusiasm or surprise.

Examples:

Congratulations on your promotion!

What a shock!

Note: Use exclamation points sparingly, to preserve their effect. If you use them liberally, they become meaningless. Also, when you do use one, stop at that—don't type two, three, or four in a row.

Periods

Besides ending a declarative sentence, a period punctuates an abbreviation.

Examples:

> *Working for the C.I.A. would be a little too exciting.*
>
> *I would rather work for the I.R.S.*

Abbreviations may also be written with no periods—**CIA** and **IRS**.

Note: When your sentence ends in an abbreviation, don't type an additional period—the period at the end of your abbreviation also ends your sentence.

Using correct punctuation is critical to communicating well with readers. Even people who don't always know how to punctuate when they write do know what punctuation means when they read. For example, they may not understand how to use a semicolon, but when they see one, they know instinctively what it signifies: that one clause has come to a halt and another is about to appear; that each clause is half of a larger statement.

How can it be that we are more knowledgeable as readers than we are as writers?

First, we have a lot more experience with reading than we do with writing. So our exposure to punctuation has been greater than our production of it. Naturally, we are better at interpreting it than we are at using it.

Second, what we know about punctuation resides largely in our unconscious because we gained a good deal of our understanding indirectly—from seeing the marks in action rather than from thinking about what they do. The information we need, as writers, does not always float to the surface on command.

Having conscious knowledge of punctuation is awfully convenient. You'll never have to scrap a sentence because you don't know how to mark it. And your readers will know what to do at every point in your text.

QUIZ ON PUNCTUATION

Below is a letter from an adolescent Noah to his parents. Your job is to edit the letter for punctuation. If a mark is wrong, correct it; if a mark is missing, supply it; if all is correct, leave it as is.

Dear Mom and Dad:

1   As you know, I had been a pretty good student in all subjects until I hit this stone wall called trigonometry. As hard as I try, I just can't seem to catch on. For many months I have been devoting five minutes a day to studying triangles, yet I still don't see the point. (Actually, there are three points and I don't see any of them.)

2   What is the use of learning trigonometry? Did either of you study it when you were in school? What in your lives requires an understanding of triangles? Is there something you haven't told me?

3 Okay, here's what I propose: home schooling. I'll get up in the morning and I'll stay home; you'll get up in the morning and you'll stay home. We won't even need to get out of our pajamas. I'll sit down; you'll tell me everything I need to know—at least, whatever you can remember. If it turns out that you know a little something about triangles, then I'll just have to hear it. How bad can it be?

4 The alternative is that I run away and live in the forest, where I'll be tutored by the animals. I'll gather them around me, one by one, maybe two by two— definitely not three by three, since that number will always remind me of trigonometry.

5 I can just imagine what you're thinking: "It's happened—he's flipped. He's always been a little strange, but this business about 'Teach me at home or I'll go live with a bunch of forest animals' is scary. Maybe we should call the school counselor."

6 Mom, Dad, listen to me: the school counselor is also the trigonometry teacher. You won't get very far with her. Instead, think about how nice it will be to sit around in our pajamas every day, just (dare I say it?) the three of us.

Noah

ANSWER TO PUNCTUATION QUIZ

There are no errors in the letter from Noah to his parents. Even though some of the marks are choices—colons can be replaced by dashes, semicolons can be turned into periods or conjunctions, parentheses can be deleted (in paragraph 1) or traded in for dashes (in paragraph 6), and so on—they are all correct.

If you thought you spotted an error, perhaps it is a punctuation choice you would not have made. Or perhaps you don't fully understand what a given mark can do. Read that part of this chapter again.

Take a moment, every week for several weeks, to focus on the punctuation in a well-written newspaper, magazine, or book. Study it; see whether you can describe the job that each mark is doing.

Start using the marks you never used before (because you didn't know how they worked).

Get feedback on your ongoing progress from someone who knows the subject well.

Don't give up—don't move to the forest. If you put your mind to it for a while, punctuating excellently will become second nature.

Index